F WALT DISNEY

NEW CONCISE N A L EDITION

THE ART OF

FROM MICKEY MOUSE

DISNEY

TO THE MAGIC KINGDOMS

BY CHRISTOPHER FINCH

HARRY N. ABRAMS, INC.
PUBLISHERS · NEW YORK

DISTRIBUTED BY
NEW AMERICAN LIBRARY

For Sarah and Justin,

for Jenny and Emily, and for Felix and Georgia

NAI Y. CHANG, *Vice-President, Design and Production*
JOHN L. HOCHMANN, *Executive Editor*
MARGARET L. KAPLAN, *Managing Editor*
BARBARA LYONS, *Director, Photo Department. Rights and Reproductions*
MICHAEL SONINO, *Abridgment*

Library of Congress Cataloging in Publication Data

Finch, Christopher.
   The art of Walt Disney.

   Bibliography: p.
   1. Disney, Walt, 1901–1966.   2. Disney (Walt)
Productions.   I. Title.
NC1766.U52D533   1975   791'.092'4 74-8435
ISBN 0-8109-9007-5

Contents

Introduction

By the time he was thirty years old, Walt Disney had become a public figure. As the creator of Mickey Mouse, his remarks—both casual and considered—were translated into dozens of languages and his likeness could be found on the pages of countless newspapers and magazines. A trim mustache and a ready smile gave him a Clark Gable-ish charm which was shared by many other young Americans of the period (as was his taste for sporty jackets and boldly patterned sweaters). What distinguished him from the rest, and made his face memorable, was a sense of determination and purpose which was apparent even in his most relaxed poses. In later years he entered our living rooms and addressed us from the television screen. By that time his face and frame had broadened and he had begun to favor conservatively cut suits and sober neckties. The mustache and the smile remained, however, as did the evident purpose and determination.

By definition, public figures are known to everyone; yet, even after talking with some of Disney's closest associates, it is impossible to escape the conclusion that *nobody* really knew him. Always there was some aspect of his personality that was just out of reach. He was a man who believed absolutely in his own instincts and abilities, an artist who would go to any lengths to ensure that a project was carried out exactly as he had conceived it. He surrounded himself with talents of every kind, but at all times he was in complete control. The master plan was in Walt Disney's head and remained unknowable until, piece by piece, it was given concrete form and grafted onto the mythology of our century.

At the outset of his career Disney was often underestimated by his rivals. They were aware of the caliber of the talents he had surrounded himself with and assumed that if these talents could be lured away, the Disney Studio would collapse. It soon became apparent that the one man who made Walt Disney Productions uniquely successful was not available at any price.

In later years Disney has been underestimated in other ways. Since the values expressed in his movies are essentially the simple values of the cartoon and the fairy story, many people have been tempted into presenting simplistic pictures of Disney the man, and of what he stood for. Some have chosen to portray him as a naive genius, while others—dazzled by the success of his varied enterprises—prefer to see him as just another business tycoon. These versions of Disney bear little relationship to any ascertainable truth. Everyone who worked closely with him admits that money was important to Disney only insofar as it enabled him to produce better movies, improve his parks, or (in later years) plan the city of the future. He was a perfectionist and perfection did not come cheap in these fields.

The notion that Disney was a naive genius is equally misleading. In his movies, right is right and wrong is wrong, but—given his background and the audience he knew himself to be in touch with—this should not surprise anyone and, although he remained faithful to uncomplicated values, he was by no means a simple man. There was much more to his success than a blind faith in intuition. He knew that for intuition to mean anything it had to be implemented, and that this demanded a combination of stringent analysis and sheer hard work, backed up by the practical talents of the artists with whom he surrounded himself. Improving the product seems to have occupied his mind night and day. After hours and on weekends he would prowl the studio—familiarizing himself with the development of every project. He subjected each decision to intensive discussion, drawing upon every available source of expertise, and there is ample evidence to suggest that he sometimes mulled over ideas for years before they were permitted to reach this stage.

Having received relatively little formal schooling, Disney went to great lengths to educate himself and his artists (at times, the old studio on Hyperion Avenue must have seemed more like the art department of some progressive university than a productive component of the motion picture industry). Disney started in the field of animated films determined to be better than anyone else. Achieving this rather quickly, he embarked on a lifelong quest to "plus" his own accomplishments ("plus," used as a verb, is a favorite word with old hands at the Studio). Throughout the thirties and into the forties, amazing progress was made in the development of the animated film. The Disney Studio gave to the world painted characters who not only moved but seemed to think for themselves. By the time of *Pinocchio* and *Fantasia*, Disney had brought to a spectacular maturity an art form that had been in its infancy just a dozen years earlier.

Disney himself was not a great draftsman, and he never pretended to be one. He was always the first to admit that, after about 1926, he did not contribute a single drawing to any of his cartoons. His great abilities lay in the area of ideas—conceiving them, developing them, and seeing them through to a successful conclusion. Ideas were commodities that he was never short of (if he ever had a problem with ideas it was that he sometimes had too many to give them all the attention that they deserved). A superb story editor, Disney worked with his artists, phrasing and rephrasing the structure of a movie until every minute action, each last nuance of character contributed to the development of the plot. This was a skill that he acquired while making the short cartoons of the early and middle thirties, cartoons which—since they ran from just six to eight minutes each—demanded the greatest economy of action. When he turned to making feature films, the same principles were applied, so that nothing that was not essential to the telling of the story ever found its way onto the screen. It was Disney's intense involvement with plot development and character, along with his uncanny grasp of technical possibilities, that gave his best movies the tightness of structure that has enabled them to survive so well in our collective memory.

He was not, of course, infallible. He did produce mediocre films and even a few that were outright failures (usually the worst failures were the ones that did not sustain his personal interest). The point is that Disney, like any other artist, deserves to be judged by his best work and he was, at his best, one of the most vigorous and innovative film-makers in the entire history of the cinema.

Animated movies are difficult to illustrate adequately. They depend on movement to achieve their effect, and a single image taken from a cartoon will often seem static and lifeless. Fortunately, the final setup that is shot by the camera is not the only art work involved in the making of an animated film. It is, in fact, the last link in an elaborate chain that includes character studies, model sheets, story continuity sketches, layouts, background paintings, animation drawings, color models, and the like. The work produced at various of these stages is often very lively. The artists who are concerned with story and layout, for example, have to sell their ideas to their director and the producer (in most instances they would be dealing with Walt Disney himself) and attempt to get into their drawings the "feel" of what will appear on screen. Thus, if Mickey should receive a shock that causes him to fall from his chair, the story artist must suggest both the shock and the fall in a single drawing (much as a book illustrator would do). The layout artist will take the same scene, provide a detailed context for the event, and diagrammatically map out the entire action. Either of these representations does, in most cases, give more of a sense of what is eventually seen on screen than does a single frame from the movie. Happily, many of these drawings have been preserved and we are able to use them here. Not only do they effectively convey the "feel" of what eventually appeared on screen; they are often very beautiful in their own right. Some appeal because of their spontaneity, others because of their attention to detail; and, beyond that, they tell us much about the way in which an animated film is conceived and executed.

Each of these drawings contains some clues to the secret of

Disney's success, since every one of them was touched by his influence. Each drawing reflects his taste, for the artist was always aware that it was subject to his scrutiny (which was far from uncritical). Literally hundreds of artists figure in this story, but all of them functioned within the governing structure elaborated by Disney's imagination. In later years he may perhaps have exercised less control over some aspects of the operation—his interests became so diversified that this was unavoidable. In the productions on which his reputation rests, however, Walt Disney's involvement was complete.

1. A new art form...

1 Early Enterprises

Walter Elias Disney was born into a modest Chicago household on December 5, 1901. His father, Elias Disney, was Canadian born and of Anglo-Irish descent. Elias was a building contractor, and we may judge the success of that operation by the fact that Walt later described how his mother sometimes went out to the building site with the men, sawing and hammering planks. At the time of Walt's birth, there were already three children in the family—Herbert, Raymond, and Roy. Walt was to develop an especially close relationship with Roy, who was nearest to him in age, a relationship that was to be of great importance to both of them. Later a daughter—Ruth—was added to the family.

In 1906, Elias Disney decided to pull up his roots once again and moved his family to a forty-eight-acre farm outside Marceline, Missouri. Small farms, then as now, did not offer an easy route to prosperity. Herbert and Raymond, both in their teens, had developed a taste for city life and soon returned to Chicago. Walt and Roy were, of course, expected to help their parents with the farm chores. It was an extremely hard life, but one which Walt later remembered with considerable affection.

It was on the farm that he began to draw. We may be sure that this was not encouraged by his parents, but he did make the first tentative steps toward his eventual career. Meanwhile, the farm operation was in trouble. In 1910, Elias sold the farm with all its livestock and moved the family once again—this time to Kansas City, ninety-five miles southwest. There Elias bought a newspaper delivery business. Naturally, Walt and Roy were co-opted into contributing their services and found themselves getting up at 3:30 in the morning to meet the trucks of the *Kansas City Star*. Despite this hard work, Walt's interest in drawing persisted, as did a growing taste for theatrical expression. In a rare gesture of indulgence, Elias Disney allowed Walt to enroll for Saturday morning classes at the Kansas City Art Institute (the elder Disney justified this on the grounds that the classes would be "educational"). Thus, at the age of fourteen, Walt acquired a smattering of formal art training.

In 1917, Elias decided upon another move. This time he returned to Chicago, where he purchased a part share in a small factory. Walt remained in Kansas City to finish out his school year

Walt Disney's birthplace at 1249 Tripp Avenue, Chicago, built by his father, Elias Disney

(Roy was still there, working as a bank teller); then he spent the summer as a news butcher on the Santa Fe Railroad (news butchers hawked newspapers, fruit, candy, and soft drinks), a job which enabled him to see a little more of the country while feeding his enthusiasm for trains—an enthusiasm which would provide him with an important outlet later in life. In the fall, he joined the family in Chicago and enrolled at McKinley High School. Here he contributed drawings to the school paper and managed to get some further art instruction from a newspaper cartoonist named Leroy Gossett. World War I was in progress and on June 22, 1917, Roy Disney enlisted in the Navy. Walt had dreams of enlisting too, but he was under age. He discovered that one had to be only seventeen to become a Red Cross ambulance driver and, though still sixteen, managed to join up (his mother, probably relieved that he would be driving an ambulance rather than handling a rifle, allowed him to falsify his birth date on the application). He was sent to a staging post at Sound Beach, Connecticut, but the Armistice was signed before he got any further. There was still, however, a need for drivers in Europe and he eventually found himself in France, assigned to a military canteen in Neufchâteau, where he soon established himself as the unit's unofficial artist, earning a few extra francs with such enterprises as painting fake medals onto leather jackets and camouflaging captured German helmets so that they could be passed off as snipers' helmets.

Disney returned to the United States in 1919. His father had a job waiting for him, but Walt was determined to make a career in commercial art. He headed for Kansas City and found work at a local studio where he made friends with another employee, Ubbe "Ub" Iwerks, a young man of Dutch descent who was to become the most important associate of his early career. Iwerks was a talented draftsman, and it soon occurred to them to get into business for themselves. They acquired desk space at the offices of a publication called *Restaurant News* and immediately achieved some modest success. But then Disney saw a newspaper advertisement for a job with an organization called Kansas City Slide Company (soon changed to Kansas City Film Ad). This company made what we would now call commercials for display in local movie theaters. They were, in fact, producing crude animated films. This new medium and the salary offered—forty dollars a week—appealed to Disney. He applied for the job and got it. Iwerks took over the business they had started, but within a few months he, too, joined Kansas City Film Ad.

The animation produced at Kansas City Film Ad consisted mainly of stop-action photography of jointed cardboard figures—a technique that precluded any serious effort toward naturalism. Nonetheless, it provided Disney, still just eighteen years old, and Iwerks with the basic training they needed. Before long, Disney

Elias and Flora Disney in 1913

Walt Disney at nine months

Walt Disney at the age of twelve

borrowed a camera and tried some animation on his own. The result was a little reel of topical gags—reminiscent in character of newspaper cartoons—which he managed to sell to the Newman Theater, a local movie house. A number of short "commercials" and illustrated jokes—known collectively as the Newman Laugh-o-Grams—were made for the theater. They dealt with such topics as shorter skirts and police corruption. Technically they were very competent by the standards of the day, and, encouraged by this initial success, Disney managed to raise enough capital to leave Kansas City Film Ad and set up on his own, retaining Laugh-o-Grams as the company's name. It might be assumed that a young man just emerging from his teens would have been content to stick with familiar material, at least for a while, but Disney was ambitious and immediately started work on a series of updated fairy tales. Six of these were made: *Cinderella, The Four Musicians of Bremen, Goldie Locks and the Three Bears, Jack and the Beanstalk, Little Red Riding Hood,* and *Puss in Boots.* The Disney archives have prints of *The Four Musicians of Bremen* and *Puss in Boots,* and they provide clear evidence that Disney was not overestimating his ability when he entered production at this tender age. *Puss in Boots,* for example, is rather well animated, and the story displays a nice sense of humor (the fairy-tale atmosphere is updated so that, for instance, the King rides around in a chauffeur-driven convertible).

In the course of producing these short cartoons, Disney began to build up an able staff which soon included, besides Iwerks, Rudolf Ising, Hugh and Walker Harman, Carmen "Max" Maxwell, and Red Lyon. Unfortunately, the Laugh-o-Grams were not selling (one sale was made but the purchaser went bankrupt after making a $100 deposit), and the Disney production team was always looking for alternate sources of income. They worked on a live-action short called *Martha* and, sponsored by a local dentist, even made a film on dental hygiene which combined live action and animation to get its didactic message across. Max Fleischer had been using this same combination in his *Out of the Inkwell* series, and it had the advantage that the live-action sections of the movies were relatively inexpensive to produce. At some time in 1923, Disney decided to try to save his Laugh-o-Grams venture by making just such a movie, in which a human heroine could cavort with cartoon characters. Rather than simply imitating Fleischer's technique, Disney hit on the idea of reversing the basic principle so that the live action would be introduced into the cartoon.

The effect of blending the real Alice with the cartoon characters was achieved by photographing a little girl named Virginia Davis against a white background and then combining this film, in the printing process, with another strip on which the animation was shot. The technique worked well, but *Alice's*

19

Poster for an Alice Comedy with the original Alice, Virginia Davis

Wonderland exhausted Disney's remaining credit and he was forced to close the studio.

He was not, however, the type to be put off by a setback of this kind, and immediately planned to restart his career. In the summer of 1923 Walt Disney, aged twenty-one, took a train to California, carrying *Alice's Wonderland* with him as a sample. His brother Roy was already in the West, recuperating in a Veteran's hospital from a bout with tuberculosis.

On arriving in Los Angeles, Disney moved in with his uncle Robert Disney at 4406 Kingswell Avenue. Walt began to look for a job and, in his spare time, used his uncle's garage to build a stand for the animation camera that he had purchased (this would have

A later Alice, Margie Gay, seen here with animated friends and with director Walt Disney

been a conventional movie camera converted to shoot stop-action).

Additions to the staff had to be made to accommodate the success of six new Alice films made in Hollywood, and one new employee was an Idaho girl named Lillian Bounds. She often worked nights, and Walt would sometimes drive her home in his car. A romance blossomed and, in July, 1925, the pair were married. Roy Disney had meanwhile married Edna Francis, his Kansas City sweetheart.

By 1927, it became evident that they had to find a replacement for the Alice Comedies if the Studio was to remain in a healthy economic state. They were by then approaching their sixtieth episode in the series, and evidently could not keep it going much longer. Apart from anything else, the use of live action placed severe restrictions on them and Walt was anxious to get back to full animation. They began work on a new series which was to be based on the adventures of Oswald the Lucky Rabbit.

Most business crises are brought on by incompetence. The near catastrophe that the Disneys faced in 1927 resulted from the very opposite. The new cartoon series turned out to be very successful, making Oswald the Lucky Rabbit a desirable property.

There was just one snag. Disney had signed a one-year contract with Charles Mintz, who had married the distributor of Disney Films, Margaret Winkler, in 1924 (their distribution outlet now tied in with Universal Pictures). The advertising announced "Oswald the Lucky Rabbit, created by Walt Disney," but—and this proved to be the fatal flaw in the contract—Oswald's name belonged to Mintz (who had, apparently, picked it out of a hat). As the first year of the series moved to a successful conclusion, Walt Disney and his wife embarked for New York, where he expected to

The series of cartoons Disney built around Oswald the Lucky Rabbit was successful enough to attract merchandising tie-ins. The model sheet below shows that Oswald anticipated some of the physical characteristics of Mickey Mouse. The page of story continuity sketches, on the right, illustrates how cartoon stories were worked out in this period

renegotiate the contract with provisions for a modest increase of income. He had kept in close contact with his distributor through George Winkler, Margaret's brother, who had made several visits to California, and there was no reason to suspect that anything was amiss. When Disney arrived in New York, however, the true reasons for Winkler's visits became painfully obvious.

Instead of offering an improved contract, Mintz actually proposed one which would entail a *reduction* of income for the Studio. This was clearly absurd, since Oswald had been very profitable. Obviously, Disney could not accept such a deal, and the reality of the situation became apparent. Mintz had decided to repossess Oswald. The character's name belonged to him, and his brother-in-law had persuaded several of Disney's best animators to take over production of the Oswald series. The motive was, of course, reduction of costs to the distributor. Mintz was the first of many people to underestimate Disney. He figured that if he could hire away Disney's best men, he would be getting the same product for a reduced outlay.

Disney was shocked and hurt by this revelation. He had trusted Mintz and he had trusted his employees. It is not hard to imagine the kinds of thoughts that must have run through his head as he and Lillian waited out the long, slow train ride back to

Original art by Hugh Harman and Carmen Maxwell for an Oswald poster

Margie Gay poses with,
left to right, Ham Hamilton,
Roy Disney, Hugh Harman,
Walt Disney, Rudy Ising, Ub Iwerks,
and Walker Harman

California. He was disgusted but not, as the next few months would prove, discouraged. His team was depleted but it still included his two most important associates—his brother Roy and Ub Iwerks (who was, by then, a partner in the business). More important still, Walt Disney had faith in his own abilities. He had reached the age of twenty-six after touching many of the bases of hardship that had come to seem archetypal of America in the first quarter of this century. His personal creed must have included the notion that success does not come easily.

This photo of the production staff was taken in 1932, after Disney had won an Academy Award—his first—for the creation of Mickey Mouse

2 Mickey Mouse and Silly Symphonies

It seems appropriate that the birth of Mickey Mouse—a creature of mythic stature—should be shrouded in legend. What we can be reasonably sure of is that the Mickey Mouse who made his debut in New York City in 1928 resulted from a collaborative effort between Disney and Ub Iwerks. It seems probable that Iwerks, easily the best animator of the day, was largely responsible for defining Mickey's physical characteristics. Mickey did bear a family resemblance to Oswald, but Iwerks—either on his own initiative or at Disney's suggestion—made the figure more compact. He was constructed from two large circles, one for the trunk and one for the head, to which were appended two smaller circles, representing ears, and rubber-hose arms and legs which terminated in plump hands (ungloved at this early stage) and large feet which gave him stability. He was also equipped with a long, skinny tail and short pants decorated with buttons fore and aft. The circular head was made expressive by the addition of a mischievous snout, a plum-shaped nose, and button eyes. He was designed for maximum ease of animation (it had been discovered that circular forms were simpler to animate effectively) but, beyond that, Mickey's identity had a dimension which was quite new in cartoons.

The gift of personality was probably Disney's own contribution to Mickey. Iwerks made the whole thing possible through his skill as a draftsman, but it was Disney's control over the situations in which the Mouse found himself that allowed this personality to develop. Even at this early date, Disney had grasped the notion that cartoon characters should seem to think for themselves. In some ways he may even have viewed Mickey as his alter ego. Certainly he always maintained a special affection for the Mouse, a fact which suggests that he was intimately involved in every stage of its creation.

The Disney brothers had managed to save enough money to go ahead with the first Mickey Mouse cartoons even without a distributor, and work began almost at once. This was carried out in secret at first, since the Oswald contract had not yet completely expired. On October 23, 1927, a bombshell had hit the motion picture industry. Warner Brothers released *The Jazz Singer* and the sound era became a reality. Lee DeForest had developed a practical sound system at least four years earlier, but the Hol-

In *Steamboat Willie*, 1928, the first cartoon to feature a fully synchronized sound track, Mickey and Minnie transform the cargo of a riverboat—including livestock—into an orchestra

lywood production chiefs had fought shy of this new development. Now they had to confront it.

As the first Mouse cartoons went into production, the industry was still in chaos. One Disney cartoon, *Plane Crazy*, had been completed, and another *Gallopin' Gaucho*, was on the drawing boards before the decision was made—perhaps the most important decision that Disney ever made. He wanted Mickey to have real impact, and he saw that the future lay with sound. What he had in mind was a cartoon in which music, effects, and action would all be synchronized.

Wedding sound to animated drawings was not, he realized, something that could be approached casually. Where live actors were concerned, it might be enough for the audience to hear them speak—that seemed like a miracle after the decades of silence (the fact that sound pictures were quickly labeled "talkies" indicates just where the public's interest lay)—but Disney did not have the ready-made stars to whom he could return the gift of speech. He had to come up with a more imaginative solution.

Les Clark, who was party to these early experiments, describes the system that was devised as follows:

"We worked with an exposure sheet on which every line was a single frame of action. We could break down the sound effects so that every eight frames we'd have an accent, or every sixteen frames, or every twelve frames. [Sound film runs through the projector at twenty-four frames a second.] And on that twelfth drawing, say, we'd accent whatever was happening—a hit on the head or a footstep or whatever it would be, to synchronize to the sound effect or the music."

By setting a metronome to correspond with the accents thus established in the action, a rough sound accompaniment could be improvised to the animation. One legendary evening, Disney and his co-workers presented a short sequence from *Steamboat Willie*—such was the title of the new cartoon—to an audience of wives and girlfriends. Roy Disney projected the film from outside a window (to eliminate motor noise), while his brother, along with Iwerks, Jackson, Clark, and a few others, improvised their sound accompaniment, live, in another room—all of them working carefully to the beat of the metronome. Jackson played his harmonica (the tune was probably "Steamboat Bill") while the others provided sound effects with cowbells, slide whistles, tin pans, and the like. This accompaniment was transmitted to the audience by way of a crude loudspeaker system set up by Iwerks. The wives and girlfriends were only mildly impressed, but the performers were convinced that they had now found the answer.

Disney went to New York. He hired Carl Edouwards, who had led the pit orchestra at the Broadway Strand and worked for the Roxy chain, to provide a band and conduct the recording session.

The first page of the *Steamboat Willie* continuity script. Disney kept this souvenir of his first major breakthrough in his office

-Main Title-

Orchestra starts playing opening verses of ' Steamboat Bill ', as soon as title flashes on.

The orchestration can be so arrainged that many variations may be included before the title fades out.

It would be best if the music was arrainged so that the end of a verse would end at the end of the title...... and a new verse start at beginning of the first scene.

MAIN TITLE

Scene # 1.
Opening effect of black foliage passing by in front of camera gradually getting thinner until full scene is revealed

Action......Old side'wheel river steamboat puddleing down stream. The two smoke stacks work up and down alternately.... shooting black chunks of smoke out as they shoot up....smoke makes stacks bulge out as it goes up and out. (16 drawing cycle) 12 Ft. from opening, the Three whistles on top of cabin squat down before they whistle tune ' TA--DA-DE-DA-DA--- DA-DA-'.....2 Ft. of action after whistle and out.

Scene # 2.
Close up of Mickey in cabin of wheel'house, keeping time to last two measures of verse of ' steamboat Bill '. With gesture he starts whistleing the chorus in perfect time to music....his body keeping time with every other beat while his shoulders and foot keep time with each beat. At the end of every two measures he twirls wheel which makes a ratchet sound as it spins. He takes in breath at proper time according to music. When he finishes last measure he reaches up and pulls on whistle cord above his head. (Use FIFE to imitate his whistle)

On September 14, Walt wrote to Roy and Ub: "We are using a seventeen-piece orchestra and three of the best trap drummers and effect men in town. They get ten dollars an hour for this work. It will take three hours to do it, plus the time the effect men put in today." Later in the same letter he says that there would be about thirty-five men on the job, but this may have included technicians. At all events, the first recording session was a disaster. Disney's team had developed a system of indicating–probably by flashes on the screen—the tempo to which the orchestra should play. Thus the film could be projected and serve the same function as a metronome. Unfortunately this system was a little crude, and Edouwards did not feel inclined to have his tempo determined by such a coarse mechanical device. Disney was forced to cable California for more money and to try again. Roy sent out enough money to proceed with a second session.

One improvement was that instead of sticking with the crude flashing device that had been used at the first session, Disney had had the film reprinted with the addition of a bouncing ball system, to indicate the accents as well as the beat, making it much easier for Edouwards to follow. Fewer musicians were used at the second

A scene from *The Karnival Kid*, 1929

A scene from *The Fire Fighters*, 1930

session, and everything went off without a hitch. *Steamboat Willie* now had a sound track and Mickey Mouse was ready for his debut.

Finding a distributor was not easy, however. Still in New York, Disney took his sound cartoon from screening room to screening room, but the industry remained in a state of confusion and the response he met was discouraging. Eventually, Harry Reichenbach, then managing Manhattan's Colony Theater, saw *Steamboat Willie* and offered Disney a two-week run.

The Mickey Mouse who hit the movie houses in the late twenties was not quite the well-behaved character most of us are familiar with today. He was mischievous, to say the least, and even displayed a streak of cruelty (which soon disappeared), but from the very beginning he had that little germ of real personality we have remarked on, and this prevented him from seeming to be just another callously cruel cartoon animal. At times—when confronted by Pegleg Pete (the perennial villain who co-starred in both *Steamboat Willie* and *Gallopin' Gaucho*), or when forced to defend Minnie's honor—he was even capable of heroic behavior. His heroism, however, was usually the heroism of the little man; it resembled the intermittent nobility of Charlie Chaplin's tramp. Chaplin undoubtedly provided Disney with one of his most important models, and we may say that Mickey and his gang provided for the sound era the kind of entertainment that Chaplin and the Mack Sennett comedians had provided for an earlier generation. Since this *was* the sound era, Mickey had to have a voice. Several people, mostly from the Studio, had a shot at immortality as the Mouse's voice, but Disney was not satisfied with any of them. He knew just the kind of squeaky falsetto Mickey should have, and it soon became clear that only he could speak for the Mouse (he continued to fill this role for twenty years).

Minnie was with Mickey from the very first. In *Steamboat Willie*, after Pete has chased Mickey from the bridge of the riverboat on which he is employed as a deck hand, Minnie is discovered on shore, about to miss the boat. The ship is already moving downstream when Mickey manages to snag Minnie's patched panties with a boat hook and haul her aboard. Later, on the deck, they cavort with the cargo of livestock, using the various animals as musical instruments on which to improvise "Turkey in the Straw."

This sequence is by far the most interesting in the movie in that it contains the seeds of much that was to come. It is also marked by a kind of humor Disney was later to abandon on grounds of taste. Mickey, for example, stretches a cat's tail so that it becomes a stringed instrument; the cat gives vocal expression to its displeasure at this misuse of its anatomy. A good deal of music and laughter is

An early Mickey Mouse model sheet which shows the basic simplicity of his design

milked out of a cow's udder (later, the Hays Office was to insist that Disney cows be udderless and, indeed, it was actively suggested that they find some suitable form of apparel). Minnie cranks a goat's tail, transforming the unfortunate beast into a hurdy-gurdy, while Mickey plays xylophone riffs on a cow's teeth (the xylophone was a much-used instrument in the sound tracks of these early shorts, providing good opportunities for visual puns; almost any more or less regular group of solid objects—the rib cage of a skeleton, for example—could double as a xylophone).

A number of new Mickey Mouse cartoons appeared in 1929, sporting titles such as *The Karnival Kid, Mickey's Choo Choo,* and *The Jazz Fool* (this last a take-off on Al Jolson). Mickey acquired, within the space of a few months, gloves, shoes, and a more endearing manner. There were other developments too. The sound tracks became increasingly sophisticated, and in most cases they were now recorded before the animators began work. That is to say, once a story line was established, a score was prepared to fit the action; it was recorded and the animators worked to the rhythms and accents contained in the sound track. This system allowed for greater flexibility.

To handle the music side of the business, Disney called in an old acquaintance from Kansas City, Carl Stalling. Stalling had had years of experience in the theater pit, providing music for silent

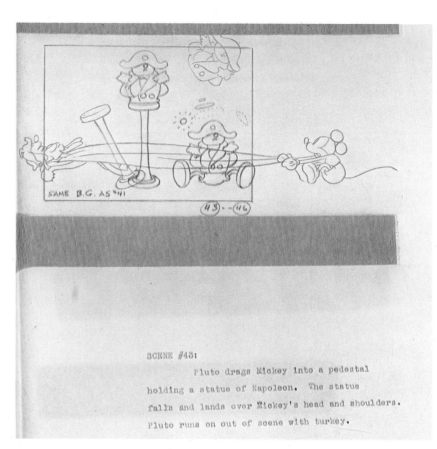

SCENE #43:

Pluto drags Mickey into a pedestal
holding a statue of Napoleon. The statue
falls and lands over Mickey's head and shoulders.
Pluto runs on out of scene with turkey.

This story sketch for *The Grocery Boy* shows how the scene is to be laid out.
Different stages of the action are indicated in a single drawing

In his early films Mickey often appeared
as an entertainer. The scene shown here is
from *Blue Rhythm*, 1931

movies—a background which left him well equipped for his new
career. Already the Disney team was becoming extremely adept at
synchronizing sound and action, and several of the earliest Mickey
Mouse pictures—*The Opry House,* for instance, and *The Jazz
Fool*—took music as the main substance of the plot.

This emphasis on music led in the same year, 1929, to quite a
new kind of animated film—the Silly Symphonies. These were to be
not merely illustrated songs, but films in which music and
animation were combined to provide a totally new experience. The
name Silly Symphonies was selected for the series, and work began
on the first of them, *The Skeleton Dance.*

The Skeleton Dance opens as cats, howling in a cemetery, are
disturbed at midnight by four skeletons who emerge from their
graves. The skeletons go through some fairly elaborate dance
sequences and then, at dawn, scurry back to their resting places.
The whole thing is set to suitable sepulchral music, a composition
of Stalling's which utilized elements from Grieg's "March of the
Dwarfs" (many film historians have erroneously reported that the
music used is Saint-Saëns' "Danse Macabre"). Despite the success

of the Mickey Mouse shorts, theater owners were a little nervous of the reception that would be accorded this new kind of cartoon entertainment, and so *The Skeleton Dance* and its successors were released under the byline "Mickey Mouse Presents a Walt Disney Silly Symphony."

These first Symphonies were received well enough for the series to continue. Certainly they were original in concept, but they now seem rather less interesting than the early Mouse shorts. Mickey gave his pictures a central core around which the action could develop. The Symphonies had no such core. Each of them

In 1929, Disney launched a new series of cartoons which he called Silly Symphonies. The first of these was *The Skeleton Dance*

From the very first, the Silly Symphonies touched a wide variety of subjects and moods. Examples illustrated here are from *The Merry Dwarfs,* 1929, and *Winter,* 1930

This camera—adapted in the late twenties to shoot animation—is still in use today

was constructed around a rather generalized theme—*The Merry Dwarfs, Winter,* and *Spring* are typical early titles—which had to be stated before it could be explored; with the techniques available in 1929 and 1930, this was quite a challenge. In a Mouse cartoon, however, you had only to catch one glimpse of Mickey to know exactly what to expect, and this allowed the animators to take much more for granted.

For the first year or two of their existence, the Symphonies had no real focus. But we must emphasize just how significant it is that Disney instituted them and then persisted with them when it would have been far easier to exploit Mickey for all he was worth. Before long, the Symphonies would have an invaluable role to play in the development of the art of animation. We should lay to rest, too, the idea that the classical music content of these cartoons showed Disney displaying pretensions toward high culture in this series. All the evidence suggests that he saw himself as making motion picture entertainment for the general public.

By the end of 1930, Mickey had become an international celebrity. Known in Italy as Topolino and as Miki Kuchi in Japan, the Mouse continued his adventures, saving Minnie from immolation by fire and worse, confronting Pete in various exotic situations, and performing to audiences of exuberant animals whose taste in music ranged from ragtime to violin concertos. A simple-minded bloodhound made an appearance in a 1930 picture called *The Chain Gang* and developed, before long, into Mickey's faithful companion Pluto. As Mickey's career unfolded in the thirties, other characters such as Horace Horsecollar and Clarabelle Cow began to enjoy the status of co-stars, but their personalities offered relatively little for the animators to work with and, as the pictures

Silly Symphony posters, 1932

became more sophisticated, their roles became less significant and eventually vanished entirely. And in 1931, Mickey was important enough for *Time* magazine to devote a feature article to him.

By the end of 1931, Disney's demand for constant improvement had driven the cost of a single cartoon to about $13,000. The Studio was barely breaking even and in 1932 another innovation drove costs still higher. In that year, Disney released a Silly Symphony called *Flowers and Trees*. This cartoon caused a sensation in the industry. It was in full color.

Technicolor had introduced a two-color system as early as 1929, but it had been used sparingly by the major studios which, with good reason, thought it had little more than novelty value (its chief limitation was that the color values were somewhat distorted). By 1932, however, Technicolor had a three-strip system ready which offered far more accurate color reproduction, and Disney at once saw its advantages. *Flowers and Trees* had been partly made as a black-and-white film. This footage was scrapped and the whole thing was done again in color. It was premiered at Grauman's Chinese Theater in Hollywood along with Irving Thalberg's production of *Strange Interlude*.

This 1932 cartoon has a special place in
the history of animation as the first to be
made in full color. From this point on, all
Silly Symphonies were produced in
Technicolor

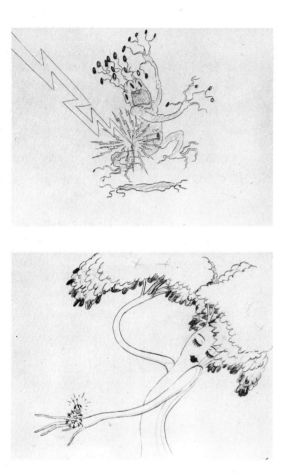

By today's standards, *Flowers and Trees* is a strange mixture of charm and absurdity. A romance between two young trees is disrupted by a crabby tree stump who initiates a fire that threatens the whole forest. Birds puncture clouds so that rain falls and douses the fire. The stump is destroyed and the two young lovers are married, with a glowworm for a wedding ring, while neighboring flowers celebrate their nuptials. Whatever weaknesses or strengths this cartoon may have had were overshadowed by the fact that it was in color. Color made it a valuable property and, from that point on, all Silly Symphonies were fully chromatic. Disney made an advantageous deal with Technicolor which gave him exclusive rights to the three-color process, as far as animation was concerned, for the next two years. For the time being, the Mickey Mouse cartoons continued to be in black and white—they were successful enough not to need the extra boost—but the Symphonies took full advantage of the new possibilities. Almost at once they became more inventive. *Flowers and Trees* was followed by *King Neptune* and *Babes in the Woods,* both of which display tighter structure and livelier action than anything previously seen in this series.

One factor which contributed to their inventiveness was the addition to the staff, in 1932, of Albert Hurter. A Swiss-born artist, he had learned the art of animation at the Barre studio in New York. From the very beginning of this association Hurter had a very special position at the Studio, Disney realizing that his gift was for producing what became known as "inspirational drawings." This is to say that he spent his time developing visual ideas for future projects and improvising on themes which might trigger the imaginations of story men or animators. Neptune's court in *King Neptune* and the gingerbread house in *Babes in the Woods* reflect his influence. He was trained in Europe and his drawings were imbued with the spirit of the gothic fairy tale. This added another dimension to the native American vigor of the Disney product. As the Studio continued to evolve, Hurter's influence was felt more and more strongly.

In 1933, Hurter designed the settings and main characters for what turned out to be the greatest Disney success up to that time—the famous *Three Little Pigs.* It is hardly necessary to recapitulate here either the plot or the success of Frank Churchill's hit tune, "Who's Afraid of the Big Bad Wolf?" The movie was a smash. Theaters retained it week after week and its impact reflects the fact that it went far beyond any of the earlier Symphonies in terms of plot and character development.

The following year, 1934, saw the production of several excellent Silly Symphonies including *The Tortoise and the Hare, The Grasshopper and the Ants,* and *The Wise Little Hen*—all of which were moral fables and showed just how proficient the Studio had become at structuring a story and establishing character. *The*

Three Little Pigs

In 1932, Walt Disney produced *The Three Little Pigs*—a cartoon which had an extraordinary impact on the American public. Its hit tune, "Who's Afraid of the Big Bad Wolf?" swept the nation

From 1932 to 1934, the Silly Symphonies evolved a new range of subtleties. Shown here are scenes from, left top to bottom, *Father Noah's Ark, The Tortoise and the Hare,* and *The Grasshopper and the Ants. Lullaby Land,* 1933, top right, presents a child's dream adventures in a landscape metamorphosed from the patchwork quilt that covers his bed. Below: *The Goddess of Spring,* from the following year

Tortoise and the Hare put Aesop into modern dress as the rakish hare loses his race to the tortoise against a milky landscape that is typical of those early color cartoons. This milkiness resulted from the fact that Emil Flohri, the Studio's top background artist, mixed a great deal of white pigment with his colors, lightening tones this way rather than by thinning his paint with water. In *The Grasshopper and the Ants,* the grasshopper is a particularly well-established character (his theme song is "The World Owes Me a Living") keyed to the voice talent of Pinto Colvig. Colvig—a former circus clown—was a musician and a member of the gag team, but his greatest claim to fame is that he provided the voice of Goofy, who had had his first supporting role in a 1932 cartoon, *Mickey's Revue.*

This layout drawing for *The Wise Little Hen,* 1934, illustrates the scene in which Donald Duck made his debut. He is discovered dancing a hornpipe on the deck of a somewhat decrepit barge, right. When the Wise Little Hen asks a favor of him, left, he feigns a tummy ache, establishing himself as a somewhat unreliable and disreputable character from the very outset of his career

The Wise Little Hen introduced another voice talent and a new character who was, within a year, to challenge Mickey as Disney's star attraction. This character was, of course, Donald Duck, and the man who provided him with a voice was Clarence "Ducky" Nash. Until Disney discovered him, Nash had worked for a milk company, entertaining children with his animal imitations. One of these imitations evolved into Donald's ill-tempered quack and made his voice known all over the world.

Donald Duck had a relatively modest role in his first screen appearance. He debuts as a miserable creature, living on a ramshackle houseboat, who feigns a bellyache every time the Wise Little Hen asks him for assistance (in this first incarnation he was drawn by Art Babbitt and by Dick Huemer, who had joined the Disney staff of animators). Donald's bill was a little longer than it is today, but he had the same voice, the same sailor suit, and the same irascible temperament. He quickly made the jump to co-starring roles in Mickey Mouse pictures such as *Orphan's Benefit,* irritating everyone on the screen but endearing himself to audiences. Many animators found the Duck difficult to work with, but two in particular—Dick Lundy and Fred Spencer—had a way with him and they must be given much of the credit for developing him into a star.

Walt looks on as Mary Moder, Pinto
Colvig, and Dorothy Compton rehearse
"Who's Afraid of the Big Bad Wolf?"
Composer Frank Churchill is at the piano

A group photograph taken at the Studio in
the mid-thirties, about the time that staff
expansion was picking up momentum

A theater marquee advertising Mickey Mouse

In *Orphan's Benefit*, 1934, Donald Duck came into his own. His efforts to entertain a group of children are frustrated by the malicious behavior of the audience, which causes him to dissolve into helpless rage

Mickey, meanwhile, had become virtually a national symbol, and as such he was expected to behave properly at all times. If he occasionally stepped out of line, any number of letters would arrive at the Studio from citizens and organizations who felt that the nation's moral well-being was in their hands. It was becoming harder and harder to find comic situations for Mickey that would not give offense in some quarter. Eventually he would be pressured into the role of straight man, but the gradual change had not yet eroded the core of his personality, and the Mouse cartoons of the mid-thirties were consistently inventive while becoming increasingly sophisticated.

3 Six Cartoon Classics

Once Hollywood had come to terms with the challenge of sound, the industry began to explore the avenues that had been opened up. The filmed musical, for instance, offered possibilities that had been totally beyond the grasp of silent cinema, and this new genre presented the theater-goer with varied and novel experiences. There were, for example, the Warner Brothers' musicals—tinseled epics like *Forty-Second Street* and *Footlight Parade*—with Busby Berkeley's spectacular choreographic symmetries punctuating the fictional show-business careers of such stars as James Cagney, Joan Blondell, Dick Powell, and Ruby Keeler. Maurice Chevalier sang his way into French high society in Rouben Mamoulian's quasi-operatic *Love Me Tonight*; the movie fan could also indulge himself, by proxy, in the silk-hat sophistication of Fred Astaire. It all helped keep the Depression at bay.

What is incredible is that, in this time of plenty in the motion picture industry, Walt Disney was able to reach a position of high eminence—matching that of the greatest stars and producers—with a modest output of animated films, none of which ran for longer than eight minutes!

Nowhere is Disney's talent as a great story editor more apparent than in the shorts of the mid-thirties. He knew how to take a simple gag situation and squeeze every last drop of humor out of it. And then he would find a way of topping that with a situation even funnier than the one preceding it.

For practical reasons, an animated cartoon is usually broken down into very short segments (different animators being assigned to each of these), so that the effect, on the screen, is of very rapid cuts from one character to another. Disney learned how to take advantage of this as a storytelling device. He badgered his story men, his layout men, and his animation directors into the realization that every cut had to be meaningful, that each short segment of the film must contribute to its overall pace. No decision was implemented without his approval, and he was constantly on hand with fresh ideas to spur flagging imaginations. Each cartoon was planned down to the last detail.

Dozens of people might be involved in this, but the entire process was controlled by Disney himself. By the time segments of action were assigned to individual animators, Disney had an almost complete knowledge of how the final product would look on the screen. The one factor that he could not control was the animation itself. Here he had to rely on the talents he had gathered around him and, by 1935, they were quite considerable.

During 1935, Disney released eighteen cartoons. At least half of them are gems. A good deal of valuable visual material has survived from this period, and this chapter is illustrated with story continuity drawings and other art work relating to six of these movies. Four of them *(The Cookie Carnival, Music Land, Who Killed Cock Robin?* and *Broken Toys)* are Silly Symphonies. *Mickey's Service Station* was the last Mouse cartoon to be produced in black and white; *The Band Concert* was the first to be made in color.

Who Killed Cock Robin?

Disney gives the old nursery rhyme a new twist. Robin, it turns out, is not dead, but has merely been wounded by Cupid's arrow.

The triumph of the cartoon is Jenny Wren, the object of Robin's passion, who is a thinly disguised caricature of Mae West

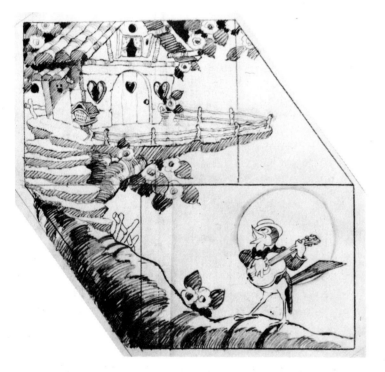

The Cookie Carnival

FROSTING FOR DECORATION

This bizarre little masterpiece is full of humorous invention. It concerns a holiday in Cookie Land, the high point of which is the election of a queen. Just as the proceedings are getting under way, a hobo cookie arrives in town, riding a boxcar in true thirties fashion. On the outskirts of the carnival he discovers a heartbroken cookie—the Cinderella of the piece—who has been left out of the parade because she does not have a suitable costume. The hobo soon remedies this with the aid of a little whipped cream and frosting and a few deftly placed candies. The transformed young lady appears before the judges and, dazzled by her charms, they declare her queen. Once she has ascended the throne, she is asked to select a consort, and she picks her hobo. The movie is so beautifully paced, and so much is packed into its plot, that it is hard to believe it lasts only eight minutes

Broken Toys

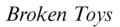

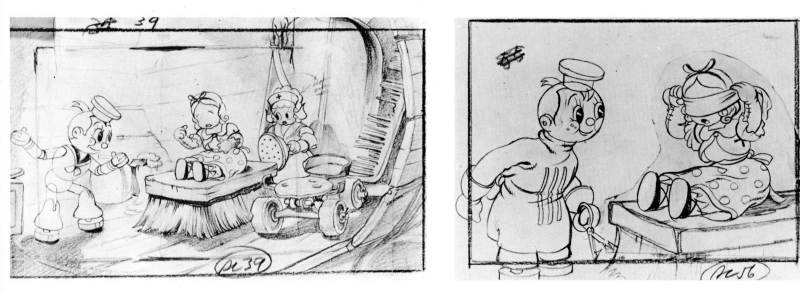

The main plot of this cartoon involves a sailor doll who performs an emergency operation to restore the sight of a dainty little creature who has lost her eyes. A neatly constructed little film, it is typical of Disney productions during the mid-thirties

Music Land

In this twist on the Romeo and Juliet story, the son of the King of the Isle of Jazz falls in love with the daughter of the Queen of the Land of Symphony. There is bad feeling between the two monarchs, and while on a clandestine visit to his sweetheart, the Prince of Jazz is captured and imprisoned. War breaks out and the Prince escapes and takes to the Sea of Discord, accompanied by his love. When both monarchs realize that their offspring are in danger of drowning, they call a cease-fire and set off to the rescue. All ends happily. The Prince and Princess are soon joined in a double wedding. A Bridge of Harmony unites the reconciled kingdoms.

In this cartoon the characters speak with the voices of musical instruments. The Land of Symphony blasts its rival with Tchaikovsky's *1812 Overture*, blowing holes in the rococo saxophone skyscrapers (see also overleaf)

Music Land

Mickey's Service Station

This was the last Mickey Mouse cartoon to
be made in black-and-white. Pegleg Pete,
the perennial villain, brings his car in for a
check-up because he has been hearing a
squeak. Mickey, Donald, and Goofy rip
the car apart looking for the source of the
offending noise. It turns out to be a cricket
which has concealed itself in the vehicle,
but our heroes do not discover this until
the car has been reduced to wreckage

The Band Concert

One of the classics of Disney animation, *The Band Concert* was the first Mickey Mouse cartoon to be made in Technicolor. Mickey is discovered in the park of a small Midwestern town, directing an orchestra in a spirited rendition of the *William Tell Overture*, but several factors conspire to disrupt the performance. A roving bee creates an irritating distraction, and, worse still, Donald Duck, in the guise of a street vendor, again and again leads the orchestra astray by playing "Turkey in the Straw" on an unending succession of fifes concealed about his person.

As the orchestra approaches the storm section of the *Overture*, a tornado approaches the town. The twister picks up the entire orchestra—along with Donald, a farm house, and assorted vegetation. Mickey doggedly continues to conduct his musicians, even as he and they are tossed about like leaves. He holds the performance together by sheer will power, and the piece comes to a rousing finale, with musicians hanging from trees and anything else that has been left standing. Mickey's triumph is ruined, however, when a fife appears from a fallen tuba and the film ends on Donald's impertinent rendition of "Turkey in the Straw"

MICK. + MUSIC PIVOTING ECCENTRIC
CORNET PIG - END OVER END.
HORSE + TYMP. PIVOTING + CIRCLING
+ LOOSE CHAIR BOBBLING UP + DOWN.

LOOKING
UP - NOT DOWN

4 Hyperion Days

On January 12, 1936, *The New York Times* published an interview headlined "H.G. Wells in Close Up." The author of *The Invisible Man* and *The History of Mr. Polly* had a few comments to make about the film industry. "Many do not realize that all Hollywood studios are so busy that they keep very much to themselves. Consequently, Chaplin never visited the Disney studios. Imagine, Charlie and Walt Disney, those two geniuses, never met! I took Charlie there. Disney has the most marvelous machinery and does the most interesting experiments. Like Chaplin he is a good psychologist and both do the only thing in film today that remains international."

Four days after the *Times* story, on January 16, René Clair was reported by the New York *Journal* as saying that the outstanding figures in the movies at that time were Charlie Chaplin and Walt Disney. "The reason is," he explained, "that they have no outside interference. They act as their own producer, director, and even attend to their own stories and musical scores. Their artistry is sublime."

On May 25, the New York *Journal* carried some outspoken opinions expressed by the composer Jerome Kern. "Cartoonist Walt Disney," said Kern, "has made the 20th century's only important contribution to music. Disney has made use of music as language. In the synchronization of humorous episodes with humorous music, he has unquestionably given us the outstanding contribution of our time. In fact I would go so far as to say it is the only real contribution."

Harper's Bazaar, dated November 1 of that same year, printed an article titled "Boom Shot of Hollywood" by Janet Flanner (better known as "Genêt"—Paris correspondent for the *New Yorker*). "Certainly the sanest spot in Hollywood," she observed, "is that studio exclusively devoted to the creation of delicate deliriums and lovely lunacies—the fun factory of Mickey Mouse, Miss Minnie and Mr. Walt Disney, Incorporated. Visitors are rarely admitted. Withdrawn to a safe distance from the rest of the movie maelstrom, the Disney plant is remotely located in one of those endless suburban settings of Barcelona bungalows, pink roses and red filling stations that makes southern California so picturesque. The studio looks like a small municipal kindergarten with

green grass for the children to keep off of and, on the roof, a gigantic glorious figure of Mickey to show them the best way.... With hysteria the seeming law for movie making, it's a wonder Mickey and Silly Symphonies succeed in this world at all, since the place where they're made is as sensible as a post office. Law and order reign there, without seeming unattractive, side by side with Minnie, Madam Clara Cluck, Donald Duck and Elmer the Elephant who, all Rabelaisian in spots but solidly moral at heart, are doubtless easier to get along with than the other big stars in the movie game."

Disney, then, did not lack for influential admirers, and the list could easily be extended. Toscanini, for example, saw *The Band Concert* six times and invited its producer to visit Italy. Sergei Eisenstein, the greatest of Soviet directors, pronounced Mickey Mouse America's most original contribution to culture.

Mickey, though still a star, was rapidly becoming a symbol, representing some concept of comedy that was to all appearances universal. In 1934 Harold Butcher, New York correspondent for the London *Daily Herald,* had written, "After a quick trip around the world ... I have returned to New York to say that Mickey Mouse has been with me most of the way. On the Pacific, in Japan and China, at Manchouli—suspended precariously between Siberia and Manchukuo. ..."

From England, in 1935, came the report that the Queen and the Duchess of York had selected Mickey Mouse chinaware as gifts for six hundred children. That same year, Mickey Mouse cartoons were used to test RCA's television system and the League of Nations voted its approval of Mickey.

Moving Day, 1936, provides Goofy with some of his finest moments, pitting him against a piano with a mind of its own. This sequence, animated by Art Babbitt, is a sustained and inspired piece of nonsense

Donald was by now seriously challenging Mickey's preeminence and, when the Studio announced his first birthday, the *New York Times* devoted a serious editorial to the growing popularity of the irascible duck, wondering if he might not replace Mickey in our affections. Dozens of other papers echoed the question.

As for Disney himself, he was learning to field the questions that come with fame. Always he was suitably modest. "I do not draw, write music or contribute most of the gags and ideas seen in our pictures today," he told the *Times.* "My work is largely to supervise, to select and shape material, to coordinate and direct the efforts of our staff."

Another reporter asked Disney how it felt to be a celebrity. "It feels fine," he replied, "when being a celebrity helps get a choice reservation for a football game. . . . As far as I can remember, being a celebrity has never helped me make a good picture, or a good shot in a polo game, or command the obedience of my daughter, or impress my wife. It doesn't even seem to help keep fleas off our dogs and, if being a celebrity won't give one an advantage over a couple of fleas, then I guess there can't be that much in being a celebrity after all."

So much for Disney the public figure, but what of Disney the man? How did his colleagues see him?

Jack Cutting, who joined the organization in 1929, recalls that Disney seemed mature beyond his years and, at times, very serious. "The people who worked best with Walt were those who were stimulated by his enthusiasm. . . . More than once, when he was in a creative mood and ideas were popping out like skyrockets, I have suddenly seen him look as if he had been hit in the face with a bucket of cold water. The eyebrow would go up and suddenly reality was the mood in the room. Someone in the group was out of tune with the creative spirit he was generating. Then he would say it was difficult to work with so-and-so."

Moose Hunters, 1937, presents Mickey, Donald, and Goofy in a series of typically disastrous confrontations with wildlife

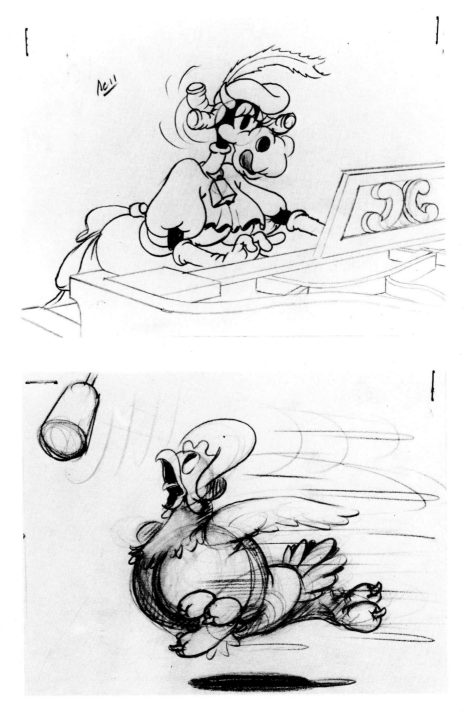

Mickey's Amateurs, 1937, offers a blend of entertainment and near catastrophe

These creative moods were often exercised at the "sweatbox" sessions which were so essential a part of the Studio routine (the projection rooms at Hyperion Avenue were not air-conditioned— hence the name sweatbox). As soon as a sequence was animated and shot as a pencil test, it would be run in one of these projection rooms. Disney would be in attendance along with animators, story men, the director, and anyone else directly concerned (sometimes people from outside the production team would be invited in to give a layman's opinion). The sequence under consideration would be subjected to an intensive analysis in an effort to see if it could be improved in any way before it was sent off to the inking and painting department. Sometimes, instead of pencil tests, it would be a "Leica reel" that would be under consideration. The Leica reel (another Disney innovation) provided a way of projecting story continuity drawings in synchronization with whatever part of the sound track had been prerecorded, thus giving at least a rough idea of how the final movie might look and sound. In any case, Disney would always lead these discussions and generally had valuable contributions to make.

Marc Davis is one of the many Disney artists who has emphasized his employer's readiness to gamble everything on an idea as one of the key factors in the growth of the Studio.

Young artists joining the Studio usually started by learning to do in-between drawings. Ward Kimball remembers that the Studio was still in a small place in those days. "The in-betweening department was down in the semibasement. . . . We called it the

A scene from *A Gentleman's Gentleman*, 1941. For a brief period during the early forties, Mickey was given ears that worked in perspective

Studying penguins as an aid to animation: standing, left to right, Walt Disney, Albert Hurter, Leigh Harline, Frenchy de Trémaudan, Clyde Geronimi, Paul Hopkins (behind Geronimi), Hugh Hennesy, Art Babbitt, Norm Ferguson, and Bill Roberts. Seated, Dick Huemer and Wilfred Jackson

bullpen and in the summer you had to strip to the waist, it was so damn hot. . . . By five o'clock I was always exhausted. . . ."

It was not every night, however, that an in-betweener could leave work at five o'clock. Apart from the overtime—which seems to have been plentiful—there were also art classes, which had become an integral part of the Studio schedule. As far back as 1931, Disney had decided that his artists would benefit from further training, and he arranged for some of them to take an evening class at the Chouinard Art School (Les Clark recalls that, since not all of them had cars, Disney himself would often drive them to school). The class these Disney artists attended was taught by a young man named Don Graham, who was soon to have an important role in the Disney organization. Graham remembers that for most of the school year 1931–32 he worked one night a week with a group of about fifteen Disney artists in his regular class.

"Walt, of course, picked up the tab. In the fall of 1932, Art Babbitt, one of the top animators at the Studio, convinced Walt that instead of sending his men across town to Chouinard, it would be far wiser to conduct classes at the Studio, where there could be more control of attendance.

"On November 15, 1932, the great Disney Art School was born in the old sound studio at Hyperion. First it was just two evenings a week, with some twenty or thirty men each evening. In a matter of three or four weeks, it became necessary to divide these classes. Phil Dike was called in and between us we worked these two evenings a week until 1934. During this period James Patrick, a talented young artist, was also employed for a few months as a teacher. The attendance during these two years averaged better than fifty men a session."

Typical of the kind of instructional material used was a book assembled by Ted Sears and Fred Moore. This contained model sheets, indicating how the main characters should be drawn, photographs of humans and animals in action poses, and detailed

A pastel drawing for *Water Babies*, 1935

A scene from *Cock of the Walk*, 1935, a Silly Symphony which includes clever parodies of Hollywood dance routines

A background painting for
Mickey's Fire Brigade, 1935

analyses of the personalities of Mickey, Donald, Goofy, and Pluto. The following, written by Sears, is a typical example:

"Mickey is not a clown . . . he is neither silly nor dumb.

"His comedy depends entirely upon the situation he is placed in.

"His age varies with the situation . . . sometimes his character is that of a young boy, and at other times, as in the adventure type of picture, he appears quite grown up. . . .

"Mickey is most amusing when in a serious predicament trying to accomplish some purpose under difficulties, or against time. . . . When Mickey is working under difficulties, the laughs occur at the climax of each small incident or action. They depend largely upon Mickey's expression, position, attitude, state of mind, etc., and the graphic way that these things are shown."

Moore added some suggestions to be kept in mind when drawing Minnie:

"Minnie seems cuter with her skirts high on her body—showing a large expanse of her lace panties. This skirt should be starched and not hang loose. . . . Her mouth could be smaller than Mickey's and maybe never open into so wide a smile, take, expression, etc.

Layout drawings for *Mickey's Garden*, left, and from *Thru the Mirror*, right

Her eyelids and eyelashes could help very much in keeping her feminine as well as the skirt swaying from the body on different poses, displaying pants. Carrying the little finger in an extended position also helps."

The following are extracts from some of Disney's comments aimed at animators who worked on a 1935 Silly Symphony, *Cock of the Walk*.

"I would suggest that you concentrate more on caricature, with action; not merely the drawing of a character to look like something, but giving your character the movements and action of the person you are trying to put over. Remember, every action should be based on what that character represents. . . .

"Something was started in this scene which is what we are striving for. This is doing things in the dance which humans are unable to do. I mean the pullet on the rooster's muscles and the juggling from side to side, but it was passed over before we had a chance to build it up into anything funny."

Seen today, *Cock of the Walk*, with its brilliant parodies of Busby Berkeley dance routines, seems one of the best cartoons of its period. In view of this, the severity of Disney's remarks seems extraordinary, but we must keep in mind the fact that he was trying to make each one of these films into a little jewel. He believed in pushing his animators as far as he would push himself. We should note, too, that he was by 1935 deeply involved in planning *Snow White* and was, therefore, very concerned with establishing the standards that would be required to make a success of his first animated feature.

60

Clock Cleaners

Mickey, Donald, and Goofy worked against this type of spectacular background in a 1937 short, *Clock Cleaners*

LEFT TO RIGHT: background paintings for a 1937
cartoon *Pluto's Quinpuplets*, for a 1939 release
Donald's Lucky Day, and for
Pluto's Dream House, 1940

Three Blind Mouseketeers

Pan shots—takes in which the action moves across a
panoramic background—necessitated elongated paintings like this one
for *Three Blind Mouseketeers,* 1936

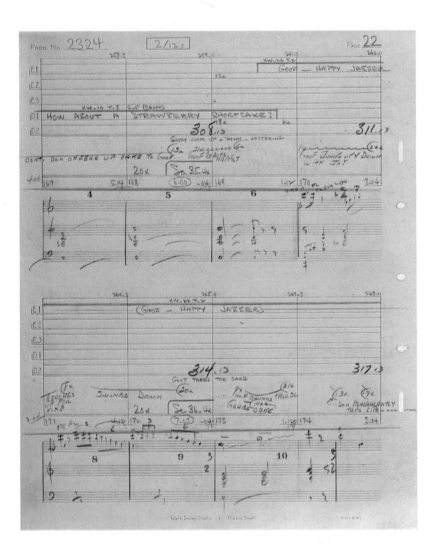

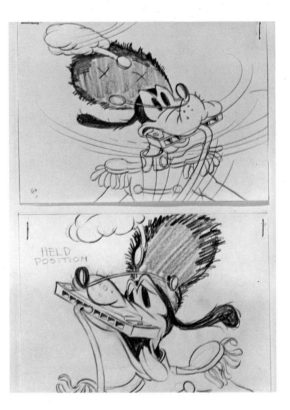

Goofy in *Mickey's Amateurs*, 1937

After a cartoon was completed, drawings were stapled into books. This group from *Fire Chief*, 1940, gives a marvelous sense of movement

Some idea of the complexity of making an animated film can be gathered from these "bar sheets," which govern the entire sound track of a movie, showing exactly where every accent should fall. At different times they have taken different forms, but this example is quite representative.

Above each bar, the film footage is noted, providing a convenient general reference. The three upper staves—E1, E2, E3—are devoted to instructions for the three effects tracks. Immediately below these—D1 and D2—are staves carrying the words to be spoken on the two dialogue tracks. A description of the action that will be seen on screen occupies the center section, along with scene numbers and other material, while the music is transcribed onto the lower half of each bar sheet

2. Feature animation...

5 Snow White: The First Feature

BASHFUL DWARF ALWAYS TYING BEARD IN KNOTS— SNOW WHITE UNTIES IT FOR HIM—

MODEL SHEET NO. 1 PROD —MO. E - 1

As *Snow White* went into production, Disney artists were asked how they thought the dwarfs might look and behave. These sketches are representative of the suggestions they made. As ideas began to clarify, model sheets were prepared

The initial success of Mickey Mouse and the Silly Symphonies did not satisfy Disney for long, and as early as 1934 he began to think seriously about making a feature-length animated film. Two important considerations prompted him to this line of thought. One was a question of simple economics, namely that no matter how successful the short cartoons were, they could never make very much money. They might share billing with the main feature—they often did—but film rental was determined by running time, not popularity, so the revenue from these shorts would always be limited. Beyond this, Disney was anxious for an opportunity to work within an expanded format—a structure that would allow for more elaborate and leisurely character development, that would give him a chance to evolve more complex plot ideas and greater naturalism. He had no intention of merely extending his established gag routines into a larger format; he was planning to take a fairy story and bring it to the screen with a kind of magical realism that was beyond the reach of live-action movies.

As everyone knows, the story Disney chose for his first feature was *Snow White and the Seven Dwarfs.* At first he referred to his new project as the "Feature Symphony," and to some extent it was an extension of the Silly Symphony concept, music playing an important part in its structure. But it was much more besides. No one can say just when Disney began to think about *Snow White,* but by the summer of 1934 his ideas were beginning to take concrete form.

An early manuscript outlines some of the dwarfs' characteristics and gives them names (narrowed down from some forty-odd previously suggested possibilities): Sleepy, Hoppy-Jumpy, Bashful, Happy, Sneezy-Wheezy—Gaspy, Biggy-Wiggy—Biggo-Ego, and Awful. These concepts and names were probably dictated by Disney. Early manuscripts also list a number of possible songs for the film—including "Some Day My Prince Will Come"—indicating that a good deal of thought had already been devoted to this aspect of the subject. Early outlines differ from the final version in a number of ways so that, for example, Snow White is envisaged passing through a whole sequence of enchanted places before the woodland animals lead her to the dwarfs' cottage. These include the Morass of Monsters and the Valley of the Dragons, which are self-explanatory, as well as Upsidedownland or Backwardland (where birds fly tail first and trees have their roots in the air) and Sleepy Valley ("vast poppy fields, slumbrous music from the wind soughing through the trees"). The Queen is described as being "stately, beautiful in the way of a Benda mask." We are told that she is cool and serene. Only in her emotional climaxes does she erupt to full fury (a note in parentheses urges study of Charles Laughton in *The Barretts of Wimpole Street).*

An outline, this one dated October 22, 1934, includes a complete breakdown of the cast of characters. We can see from this how quickly things were beginning to develop: "SNOW WHITE: Janet Gaynor type—14 years old. THE PRINCE: Doug Fairbanks type—18 years old. THE QUEEN: A mixture of Lady Macbeth and the Big Bad Wolf—Her beauty is sinister, mature, plenty of curves—She becomes ugly and menacing when scheming and mixing her poisons—Magic fluids transform her into an old witchlike hag—Her dialogue and action are overdramatic, verging on the ridiculous. THE HUNTSMAN: A minor character—Big and tough—40 years old—The Queen's trusted henchman but hasn't the heart to murder an innocent girl. . . . PRINCE'S HORSE: This gallant white charger understands but cannot talk—like Tom Mix's horse Tony—The Prince's pal. MAGIC MIRROR: The Queen's unwilling slave—Its masklike face appears when invoked—It speaks in weird voice."

This outline also includes another set of descriptions of the dwarfs—not dissimilar to the earlier one except that the names have become more settled. Already they include Happy, Sleepy, Doc, Bashful, and Grumpy. Sneezy has been temporarily ousted by Jumpy, and Dopey has yet to be christened.

By the fall of 1934, then, the cast was already pretty well established in Disney's mind. A story team was being built up, and we may presume that Albert Hurter and Joe Grant were beginning to work on character design. Very soon more detailed outlines began to circulate—mimeographed sheets that dealt with specific scenes and situations. These kept everyone in touch with progress and doubled as invitations to submit ideas and gags that would contribute to the development of the plot; within a matter of three or four months, *Snow White* had developed from the embryonic stage and was beginning to take shape as a viable endeavor.

The story at least was taking form. There was, however, a great deal more than story involved in a pioneering project of this kind. The Disney artists would be dealing with problems that neither they nor anyone else had confronted before.

There were, to start off with, several purely technical problems. All animation drawings up to this point had been made on sheets of paper measuring 9½ by 12 inches—layouts and backgrounds also being geared to these dimensions. The drawings were

Albert Hurter's studies—as in this one of the Queen after she has transformed herself into a hag—were vital to the concept of the story that began to emerge

then traced and painted onto "cels"—celluloid sheets of the same size—and sent to the camera department, along with the appropriate backgrounds. The camera could be adjusted to photograph the entire setup—minus the margins—or a small part of it if a close-up effect were required. The area to be photographed was designated as the "field" (rectangles drawn on many of the layouts illustrated in this book are indications of field size). The size of the animation paper determined the largest possible field size, which was known as "five field." As soon as production of *Snow White* got underway, it became evident that this field size would be inadequate for much of the animation involved. A scene in which Snow White was to appear with all seven dwarfs, or with fifty animals, would—if they stuck with the old animation paper—mean that each character had to be drawn on a minute scale, making the animator's task extremely difficult, if not impossible. To overcome this problem, a new field size—"six-and-a-half"—was introduced, which meant that a complete new series of animation boards, sliding cel boards, checking boards, and inking and painting boards

The Wicked Queen consults her Magic Mirror

The Huntsman falls to his knees before Snow White

Snow White is introduced in one of the film's opening scenes scrubbing the courtyard of her stepmother's palace

The Queen entrusts her huntsman with the task of murdering Snow White. Once in the forest, however, he is overcome by the princess's innocence and drops to his knees to beg her forgiveness. Clever use of shadows and camera angles adds to the drama of the scene

As Snow White flees into the forest, trees and fallen logs become monsters that seem to threaten her. The Disney artists tried to see the world through her frightened eyes, turning it into a nightmare

The woodland creatures lead Snow White to the dwarfs' cottage in a clearing in the wood

had to be designed, built, and installed; and animation cameras had to be adapted to shoot this new field size. Even so, certain long trucking shots demanded characters who would appear so small on the screen at some point that even this modification would be inadequate to the animator's needs. To get around this, a method of reducing drawings photographically was devised—a mechanical solution that allowed the artist to work on a convenient scale.

Another limitation that animation had run up against was its inability to produce a real illusion of depth. When a camera moved into a setup which consisted of a painted cel held tightly against a flat background, scale distortions were inevitable. Take, for example, a situation where a character stands in a meadow with mountains in the background. In reality, as one approaches that character he will appear to become bigger, but the mountains will remain about the same size because they are so far away. When the camera moves in on a flat representation of the same scene, both the character and the mountains will appear to increase in size at exactly the same rate. In the short cartoons this had not presented a serious problem because such situations seldom arose, and when a little distortion did creep in it was not really noticeable in the context of quick-fire gags that were sweeping the audience along; but feature films required a much greater regard for naturalism. Flat backgrounds might still be adequate for most scenes, but from time to time a real illusion of depth would be necessary. William Garity, head of the camera department, was given the job of developing a multiplane camera—one that could shoot simultaneously several layers of action and background, layers that were separated in such a way as to produce an accurate sense of depth.

Layout also presented new problems and the layout team, headed by Hugh Hennesy and Charles Philippi, found itself confronted with a considerable challenge. Layout artists not only determine the spaces in which an animator must work, they are also in a sense responsible for deciding how the film will look when it reaches the screen. They take on many of the tasks which in a live-action movie would be handled by the art director, the director of photography, and the film editor. An animated film must, in effect, be edited in advance, since animation is so costly that one cannot afford to shoot a single bit of extra footage. Every cut is determined at the layout stage (with the collaboration of the director and, sometimes, the story team). Camera angles and lighting are also determined in layout, as are final decisions about the character of the setting in which the action is to take place. This art direction aspect was especially important in *Snow White*, where it was necessary to maintain an atmosphere of fairy-tale quaintness. Most of the preliminary work to this end was done by Albert Hurter—the bizarre furnishings in the dwarfs' cottage, for instance—but it was the layout artists' responsibility to make these

The animals help Snow White to clean up the appalling disorder in the dwarfs' cottage

inventions work within the final context of the film. Color was an important consideration. In the interiors, it was keyed down to give them an aged look (Gustaf Tenggren's elegant watercolor studies had an important influence on their eventual appearance). Everything had to be carefully designed so that the characters would read clearly against their backgrounds.

By the spring of 1936, production of *Snow White* was in full swing. Story conferences were being held almost every day and each scene was discussed and analyzed down to the last detail. Live actors were also filmed as an aid to animation. The problem with animating humans is that everyone instinctively knows how a man or a woman moves, so that the least inaccuracy in the way they are drawn is immediately apparent. Nobody has ever seen a real-life Mickey Mouse, or even a real-life Dopey. Snow White, however—as well as the Prince and the Queen—presented a different kind of challenge. Years earlier, Max Fleischer had devised a method of filming live actors and using the results as a guide for his animators. This system, known as rotoscoping, yielded gestures and mannerisms that could never be invented. Now actors were brought to Hyperion Avenue (the young lady cast as Snow White went on to achieve fame as the dancer Marge Champion), and they would act out a piece of "business" in front of the cameras—often under the direction of the animators themselves. This action would then be transferred to a series of photostats which the animator could use for reference. The artist could, in fact, have simply traced the figures from the photostats, but this was seldom done because the characters had to be adapted in order to be consistent with the remainder of the animation. Instead, a kind of gentle caricature was employed, so that gestures and poses became slightly exaggerated. This system served the animators well, and they continued to use it in later movies.

Although much of the production work on *Snow White* was jammed into the final ten or twelve months, it was the result of more than three years of concentrated effort by Disney himself—three years in which he faced new problems almost daily. The whole venture was an enormous gamble from the very first. The industry was convinced that he had bitten off more than he could chew, and hints of impending disaster were commonplace in both the trade papers and the national press. During this period, the Studio staff expanded to more than one thousand, many of whom were directly involved in the feature project. Some names have been mentioned, but literally hundreds of other artists and technicians were involved in all kinds of capacities, from painting backgrounds to devising special effects. (How, for example, do you make a painted stream look like a stream, or a rain storm look like a rain storm?)

Finally, at a cost of close to $1,500,000, *Snow White* was completed. Four days before Christmas, 1937, it was premiered at the Carthay Circle Theater in Hollywood. The audience was studded with celebrities. It was the kind of opening of which Disney had always dreamed. The reviews were sensational. *Snow White*, justifying all of Disney's hopes for it, was an overnight success—impressing itself on the imagination of the Western world.

Snow White is distinguished by two seemingly opposed characteristics: economy of construction and extravagance of invention. As we have already observed, Disney's training in the field of cartoon shorts had taught him how to tell a story without wasting a single foot of film. There is nothing in *Snow White* that does not contribute either to developing character or to moving plot. (Two scenes—the dwarfs eating soup and building a bed for Snow White—were deleted at the last moment.) Yet this does not lead to a feeling of spareness, because crammed into this framework is a

Backgrounds were painted in low-keyed colors to emphasize the antique character of the cottage. *Snow White* was the only feature in which transparent colors were employed for the background paintings. Later, gouache became the usual medium

At the mine, Dopey places two huge diamonds over his eyes like spectacles. The diamonds' facets create this frightening image

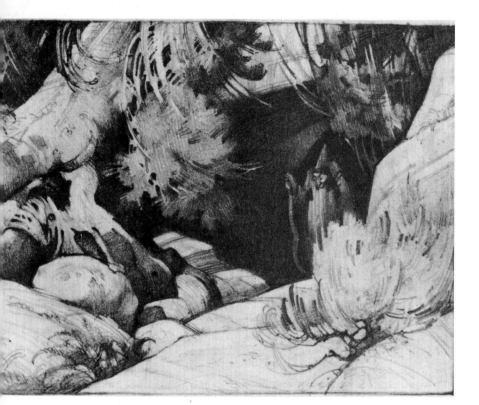

Grumpy says: "THE QUEEN! SHE'LL KILL HER!
WE'VE GOT TO SAVE HER"

Warned that the Queen (who has used magic to transform herself into an old hag) has reached her victim, the dwarfs set off to the rescue. They are too late to save Snow White, who has already bitten the poisoned apple, but they pursue the Queen up into the mountains, where a storm is raging

The Queen attempts to send a boulder crashing down on the dwarfs, but lightning strikes the crag she is perched on and she is hurled to her death

The dwarfs return to the lifeless body of Snow White and sadly place it in a crystal casket. She remains there through a full cycle of the seasons until, finally, the Prince arrives to wake her with a kiss

profusion of detail that is almost overwhelming. The fruits of three years' work by hundreds of talents are compressed into eighty-three minutes of action, imagery, music, and dialogue.

The songs are memorable and, like everything else, contribute to the movement of the story. As for the animation, the character of each dwarf is firmly established—each is a distinct individual. The development of the Queen is excellent, both before and after her transformation into the witchlike crone. The Huntsman is effective and the birds and animals function well as a kind of Greek chorus. Snow White occasionally seems a little too much like a twentieth-century co-ed, but she has great charm and easily wins our sympathy. The only real failure is the Prince, who seems wooden and lacks character (Snow White deserves a better consort). Above all, the entire movie manages to sustain the ambiance of timeless-ness which is so essential to the fairy-tale genre.

6 Pinocchio

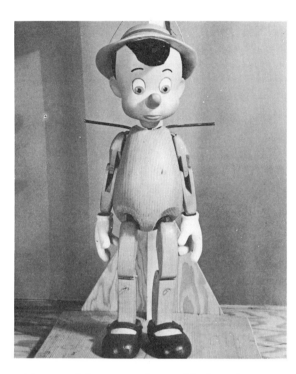

Many models were made to guide the animators

Snow White may have provided Disney with his finest moment, but *Pinocchio* is probably his greatest film. It shares in all the qualities that made the first feature such a success, and adds to them a technical brilliance which has never been surpassed.

Pinocchio opens with a stunningly effective shot—the camera pulling back from a large white star, panning across the tiled roofs of a sleepy European village, then closing in on the lighted window of Geppetto's cottage. It is the kind of shot that has become familiar enough in live-action movies since the advent of power-operated zoom lenses, but taken within the context of its own period, and within the history of animation, it is innovative and spectacular. Nor is it just a piece of flashy showmanship. It serves to capture our imagination and draw us into the atmosphere of the story before a single word has been spoken.

Disney's early success had resulted from his grasp of the potentials of the sound film. By the time of these first feature films, he had evolved a method of storytelling which relied primarily on visual means. Next to animation itself, camera movements provided his team with its chief narrative devices. Disney continued to make expert use of music and sound, but his greatest achievement was the creation of a visual language that was totally convincing and extremely flexible.

As we have seen, *Snow White* developed gradually. Now Disney seems to have felt that with the experience of one feature behind him, he need not be quite so cautious, and production of *Pinocchio* was put into top gear. Things did not work out according to plan, however, and after six months he called a halt to the project and put everyone on new assignments until the problems had been ironed out.

The primary dilemma centered on the character of Pinocchio himself. Should he be treated as a puppet or as a small boy? Until this issue was settled, very little could be done. Book illustrations of the story tended to show Pinocchio as essentially puppet-like, and this seems to have influenced the animators' first efforts. Frank Thomas, Milt Kahl, and Ollie Johnston were assigned to the character, and they animated about 150 feet of film, using the speeded-up voice of Ted Sears as a sound track. Disney was not happy with the results. After further experimentation, they went

This panoramic
background was painted
for the opening of
Pinocchio

One of Gustav Tenggren's
watercolor studies for
Pinocchio

Geppetto's workshop

At the beginning of *Pinocchio*, the Blue Fairy brings the hero to life and appoints Jiminy Cricket to be his conscience

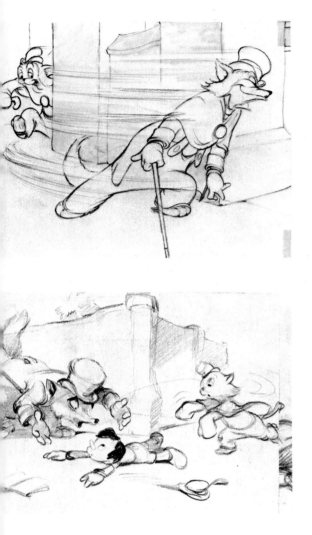

Geppetto, delighted with his new son, sends Pinocchio off to school. Before he gets there, however, Pinocchio is sidetracked by the Fox and the Cat, who persuade him that the theater offers more glamour

ahead with a more boylike version of Pinocchio (except in the scenes, animated by Thomas, where he is still on strings), and found a child's voice which fitted with this interpretation. A further snag was Jiminy Cricket's personality, which became more and more important as the story developed, until he had usurped many of the functions intended for Pinocchio.

Jiminy Cricket, animated by Ward Kimball, Woolie Reitherman, and Don Towsley, presented another kind of challenge. Being a very small character (his physical size contrasts with the importance of his role in the film) made him difficult to deal with except in close-ups. The animators rose to the challenge, making him so expansive a character that he seems larger than life. In contrast to the Cricket stands one of the villains of the piece, the puppet master Stromboli. Stromboli, animated by Bill Tytla, is an enormous, muscular presence who fills the screen with his infamy. His every gesture is a threat. Tytla was an exceptionally gifted animator, and this was an ideal assignment for him. It is probable that no one else could have built this character to the same point of menace.

Perhaps more likable, but in the villains' camp nonetheless, are the Fox and the Cat, who are slyly determined to lead Pinocchio astray for the sake of a fast buck. Animated by Norm Ferguson and John Lounsbery, these characters—like Stromboli—seem to be in constant motion, but it is motion less governed by rage. The cunning of the Fox and the stupidity of the Cat turn them into a kind of vaudeville team that keeps moving to hold the attention of the audience. The Fox knows just when to throw a knowing glance and the Cat is a malicious innocent with an instinct for mischief.

Geppetto, handled largely by Art Babbitt, is the least interesting of the main characters. He is asked to function on a single, fundamentally sentimental emotional level, thus presenting the animator with very little challenge. Fred Moore was luckier in his assignment, treating Lampwick, the cocky street kid, as something of a self-caricature. Monstro the whale is suitably fearsome and two smaller creatures, Figaro the kitten and Cleo the goldfish, add a touch of charm to the proceedings. Live-action footage was shot as an assist to the animation of several characters, notably the Blue Fairy, whose brief appearances are very effective.

Once again, Hurter's influence is felt throughout the film, both in terms of character design and in the profusion of quaint detail that crowds the background of almost every scene. Gustav Tenggren contributed many line-and-wash studies which greatly affect the look of the movie. The multiplane camera and the visual complexity of the film as a whole presented the layout team with great opportunities which they eagerly seized. Under the direction of Charles Philippi and Hugh Hennesy, with important contributions by Ken Anderson, the art of layout was carried to new heights of inventiveness. Many of the layout drawings are extremely

Stromboli shuts Pinocchio in a wooden cage. The Blue Fairy rescues him, but not before he tells her a series of lies—only to discover that, with each lie, his nose grows longer and longer, eventually sprouting branches and leaves

Chastened by his experiences, Pinocchio sets out to find Geppetto—a search which takes him under the sea. LEFT: Pinocchio being swallowed by Monstro the whale. BELOW: Jiminy Cricket and Monstro's eye. RIGHT: eventually Pinocchio and Geppetto are reunited in Monstro's belly. Escaping from the whale, who gives furious chase, Pinocchio is washed ashore, seemingly dead. But he recovers, and, having proved himself brave, truthful, and unselfish, is soon changed into a real boy by the Blue Fairy. Joyfully, Figaro the kitten dives into the fishbowl and kisses Cleo the goldfish

beautiful, and the same can be said of the background paintings. For *Snow White*, backgrounds had been painted mainly with transparent washes, but in the case of *Pinocchio*, while something that *looks* like a classic watercolor technique is adhered to, opaque pigment came into general use. For multiplane shots, all but the bottom layer was painted onto glass, and oil paint was used for this purpose.

Many character models, some fashioned from clay and some from wood, were made to assist the animators. The artist could refer to these models, turning them so that they could see at a moment's notice just how Jiminy Cricket, for example, would look

The layout drawings for *Pinocchio* were made with great attention to detail

The atmosphere of *Pinocchio* owed a great deal to the effectiveness of the background paintings, some of which are reproduced above and on the following pages

from such an angle (in this respect the models served a purpose similar to that of the live-action footage, and they could be used for characters who could not be shot in live action). The special effects in *Pinocchio* are particularly striking. Live-action rain is incorporated into one scene, for example, and one cannot overlook the impact of the musical score, highlighted by such songs as "Give a Little Whistle" and "When You Wish upon a Star"—both composed by Leigh Harline with lyrics by Ned Washington.

The plot of *Pinocchio* required extensive adaptation to make it suitable for the screen—far more radical changes than were necessary for *Snow White*. Disney was charged with frightening

children, but compared with Collodi's original, his version of *Pinocchio* is quite restrained. He kept just enough of the element of horror to make the story effective—certainly the scene in which Pinocchio's nose grows longer as a result of each of his lies triggers a deep response, as does the sequence in which he and Lampwick are transformed into donkeys.

Although the reviewers welcomed it with enthusiasm, *Pinocchio* was not an immediate box-office success. The film was released in February, 1940, five months after the outbreak of war in Europe, and it may be that the public was not in the mood for a fable of this sort. Not that *Pinocchio* was a frivolous movie. On the contrary, despite the happy ending, it presents the blackest vision of any Disney feature. But perhaps the reality of world events had made the fabulous temporarily redundant. To this day, *Pinocchio* has never reached the numbers of people who have seen some other Disney films. This is unfortunate, for it is Disney's masterpiece.

Operating the multiplane camera crane. The technician at the upper left is Card Walker, now president of Walt Disney Productions

ABOVE: shooting live action for *Fantasia;* BELOW: Stokowski in the Disney paint laboratory

7 Fantasia:
The Great Experiment

The new emphasis on feature film production did not mean that Disney had lost his special affection for Mickey Mouse, but Mickey was losing ground to Donald and this prompted Disney, in 1938, to plan a comeback for him. The vehicle he chose for this purpose was *The Sorcerer's Apprentice*, an ancient fairy-tale motif which Goethe had used in a very popular poem; Disney's immediate inspiration was Paul Dukas's orchestral work of the same title, written in 1897. This popular piece of program music seemed to provide Disney with the perfect score for his project. Its running time made for a film about twice the length of the average cartoon short, thus allowing for leisurely storytelling and substantive character development. Disney, anxious to lend this production as much prestige as possible, was fortunate enough to obtain the services of Leopold Stokowski. Stokowski, who conducted the Philadelphia Orchestra, had long admired Disney's work and was delighted to make himself available. In fact, he involved himself so intensely in the project that it soon began to develop into something far more ambitious.

The idea that evolved was for a full-length feature film which would take the form of a concert of orchestral pieces conducted by Stokowski and illustrated by the Disney artists. It had been decided that a narrator would be needed to link the various episodes of the film, and Deems Taylor, known to millions as music commentator on the Metropolitan Opera radio broadcasts, was chosen for this role and to assist in the process of selection.

Eventually, the field was narrowed down to seven main parts, the first being an introduction which culminated in Stokowski's orchestral arrangement of Bach's *Toccata and Fugue in D Minor.* Next came excerpts from Tchaikovsky's *Nutcracker Suite;* then came *The Sorcerer's Apprentice,* followed by Stravinsky's *Rite of Spring.* The fifth piece was Beethoven's *Sixth Symphony,* the "Pastoral." Then came "Dance of the Hours" from Ponchielli's opera *La Giaconda.* The final selection combined Moussorgsky's *Night on Bald Mountain* with Schubert's "Ave Maria."

The concert character of the movie as well as the fact that Stokowski and Deems Taylor were associated with it raised high expectations, and Disney went to great lengths to live up to these. He planned the movie for a special wide screen, but had to

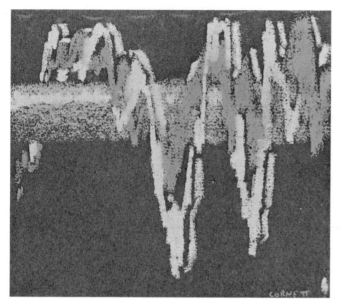
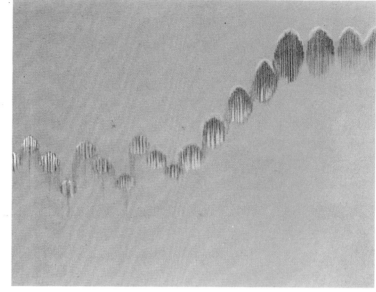

Toccata and Fugue

Hundreds of pastel studies were made for the *Toccata and Fugue* segment of *Fantasia* and for the "sound track" interlude, both of which used abstract forms to illustrate musical ideas

abandon this scheme for financial reasons. He also developed a sound system utilizing seven tracks and thirty speakers, which not only anticipated stereophonic sound but was, in fact, far more ambitious than anything that has been used since. Stokowski handled the sound mixing personally, and the results were, to judge by contemporary accounts, quite spectacular. Unhappily, the system was prohibitively expensive and was installed only in a few first-run theaters. The version of *Fantasia* that we are familiar with today has been remixed for more conventional equipment.

The film opens with a brief introductory section in which Deems Taylor sets the scene; then the *Toccata and Fugue* begins. Visually, this segment provided a field day for the Disney effects department (as did a later interlude which introduced the sound track as a character). When *Fantasia* was in production, more than sixty people worked for the effects department, and they were given the task of interpreting the patterns of Bach's music in terms of abstract and semiabstract forms. This was a new area of experiment for them and, in the circumstances, they did a creditable job, since this opening section of the movie does command one's attention and was a bold attempt to do something that had not been done before.

The *Nutcracker Suite* is ballet music, and Disney's artists treated the section of film it underpins as a kind of animated dance sequence. The first two movements of the suite were dropped and the order of the others rearranged so that a continuous story could be constructed.

A technical tour de force, the *Nutcracker Suite* section features some extraordinary animation and picks up on the romantic flavor that had colored so many of the Silly Symphonies, transforming

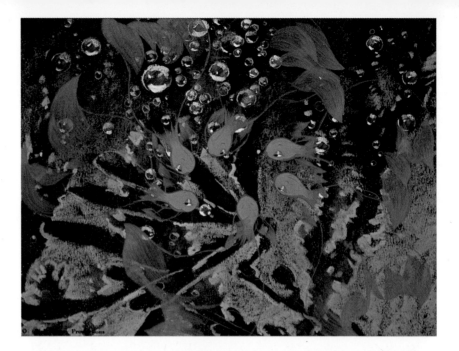

Nutcracker Suite

Disney artists transformed Tchaikovsky's *Nutcracker Suite* into a nature ballet featuring spectacular effects animation and delicate airbrush work

that sensibility into something substantial enough to provide a base for bravura performances by all concerned.

Disney had planned *The Sorcerer's Apprentice* as a spectacular showcase for Mickey and it became exactly that, the whole project being developed with great care and attention to detail. Under Jim Algar's direction, nothing was left to chance. Story sketches were made in full color and some of the Studio's top animators were put on this assignment (Bill Tytla, for example, and Les Clark, who had been drawing Mickey for ten years).

Mickey is portrayed as a young magician, the disciple of a great Wizard who, bored for the moment with his own powers, leaves Mickey in charge of the subterranean cavern where he practices his sinister craft. Mickey has been ordered to fill the large water vat in the cavern, but the ambitious apprentice discovers that the Wizard has left his magic hat behind and Mickey decides to take advantage of this. Donning the hat, he brings a broom to life and directs it to carry the water. The broom marches to the well, fills a wooden pail with water, and starts on its appointed task. Satisfied with the success of his spell, Mickey settles down in the Wizard's chair to take a snooze. Soon he is dreaming that he is high above the earth, far out in space. His powers have become so great that he can control the paths of stars and planets, and comets change their course at his bidding. Next he is standing on top of a towering crag, conducting the waves of the ocean. With a gesture worthy of Stokowski, he beckons to the breakers to smash against the base of the rock. He repeats the gesture and the waves break over the top of the crag, drenching the dreaming apprentice and startling him from his reverie.

He wakens to find that the cavern is awash. The broom is following his instructions with too great a zeal and has already brought thousands of gallons of water from the well and threatens to cause a disastrous flood. Mickey orders it to stop but his magic powers have vanished and the broom mechanically continues its task. In desperation, Mickey attacks it with an axe, only to see the broom split into many brooms, all of which continue with dogged perseverance, sweeping him aside and swamping the cavern. The water gets deeper and deeper. Furniture is afloat. Mickey seeks safety on a gigantic book of spells, which is soon sucked into an iridescent whirlpool. The apprentice seems on the point of losing his life when, suddenly, the Wizard appears at the top of the stairway. A single gesture from him and the waters subside. Everything returns to normal. Mickey, chastened, is left to clean up the mess.

Although told in an amusing way, *The Sorcerer's Apprentice* presents psychological ideas that are very basic to the human condition. Technically, like everything else in *Fantasia*, the segment is superb.

*The Sorcerer's
Apprentice*

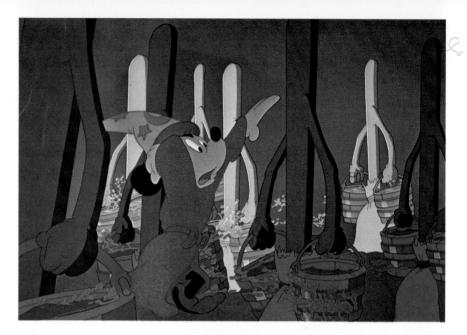

The Sorcerer's Apprentice

The Sorcerer's Apprentice presents Mickey as a neophyte magician dabbling with spells he cannot control

Rite of Spring

In *Fantasia*, Stravinsky's *Rite of Spring* is used to underscore the story of the earth's prehistory, including the age of the giant reptiles

The Rite of Spring heralds an abrupt change of mood. Disney saw Stravinsky's ballet music as providing the score for nothing less than a portrayal of the creation of the world (and certainly the insistent rhythms are suggestive of primeval forces). It begins with visions of a time when the earth was still a molten mass, and it carries the story of evolution to the point at which the dinosaurs disappeared from the face of the planet. Millions of years are telescoped into a few minutes. We see mountain ranges thrown up by gigantic volcanic convulsions; then primitive forms of marine life emerge from the oceans and learn to live on dry land. Later, huge reptiles roam the surface of the earth and engage in titanic battles to the death. Eventually, a massive drought turns whole continents into deserts.

The next segment, set to the "Pastoral" Symphony, is difficult to judge objectively. It has considerable charm, yet its visual character seems to have very little to do with the real nature of Beethoven's music.

This segment owes a great deal to the stylized decorative and illustrative idioms of the thirties—it passes before the viewer like an

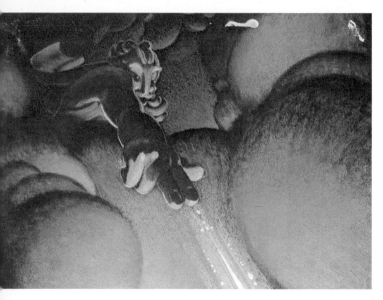

Pastoral

The version of the "Pastoral" that reached the screen owed a good deal to Art Deco idioms

Dance of the Hours

"Dance of the Hours," as interpreted by the Disney artists, became a hilarious parody of classical ballet

animated mural for some fashionable Parisian restaurant. The backgrounds are extremely elegant and pleasing, combining gently curving forms with an innovative use of color.

Good comic interludes are provided by Ward Kimball's Bacchus and his drunken unicorn-mule; toward the end, Zeus, aided by Vulcan, stages a thunderstorm for his own amusement. Night falls and Artemis appears in the sky to launch an arrow of starfire from the bow of light formed by the crescent moon.

It is difficult to give an adequate idea of Disney's interpretation of "Dance of the Hours," but we might begin by saying that it is possibly the best—and certainly the funniest—segment of the movie. The animators, who included John Lounsbery, Howard Swift, and Hugh Frazier, were given the task of developing a parody of classical ballet featuring hippos, elephants, ostriches, and alligators. The result is hilarious. A hippo in a negligible tutu does pirouettes as though she weighed no more than a feather. Alligators swoop down from behind pillars, the inherent menace of their species amplified by choreographic fantasy and clever camera angles. Elephants hide timidly behind flimsy architectural elements and ostriches perform *entrechats* with an inspired absence of grace. Gravity and reason are denied in a triumph of insanity. Directed by T. Hee and laid out by Ken O'Connor, "Dance of the Hours" is a classic of comic animation.

Fantasia concludes with *Night on Bald Mountain* and "Ave Maria." As technical achievements they are extraordinary, but emotionally they are unsatisfying. The concept of this segment is a simple

Night on Bald Mountain

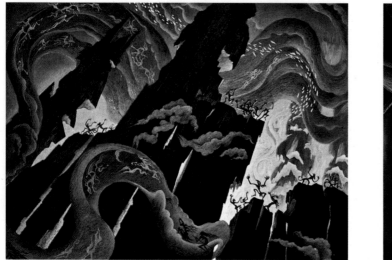 

contrast of good and evil. To Moussorgsky's dramatic music, witches ride and tormented spirits rise from the grave to join the Devil on top of a jagged, rocky peak. The special effects in these sequences are excellent and Bill Tytla's Devil is realized with enormous vigor. At dawn, the ghosts return to their resting places and, to the strains of "Ave Maria," a procession moves slowly toward a Gothic-cathedral forest of huge trees.

Fantasia is a film with great merits and great faults. Structurally it owes very little to anything that preceded it in the history of the cinema (*Snow White* and *Pinocchio* were basically conventional narratives), and Disney deserves great credit for breaking so boldly with precedent. His artists deserve credit for some of the finest animation that has ever reached the screen. *Fantasia* is an amazing piece of film-making, one that will continue to fascinate audiences.

Dumbo learns to fly

8 Dumbo and Bambi

Cinematically, *Snow White, Pinocchio,* and *Fantasia* were block-busters. The two features that followed—*Dumbo* and *Bambi*—were a little different in character.

Like *Pinocchio, Fantasia* did not have a great financial success at the time of its first release, and *Dumbo* was conceived as a way of recouping some of the losses. It was made for only a fraction of the cost of the two preceding releases, yet its earning potential would be at least equal to theirs. Multiplane shots and other expensive effects were kept to the bare minimum that would assure good production values, and the story was told as simply and directly as possible, with the emphasis placed on humorous character development. In many respects this represented a shift back to the spirit of the cartoon shorts. After the demands of the first three features, *Dumbo* was practically a vacation for the Disney artists, and they clearly enjoyed themselves on this project. It is probably the most spontaneous animated feature that the Studio has ever produced. Audiences responded well to it and the film brought in much-needed revenue (only the fact that its release antedated Pearl Harbor by less than two months prevented it from having an even greater impact).

Dumbo, as everyone knows, is the story of a baby elephant who discovers that he can fly. Adapted for the screen by Joe Grant and Dick Huemer, the film has a number of highlights. The circus parade and the scenes with Dumbo and the clowns have a splashy vigor spiced with the kind of knockabout humor that benefited greatly from the expertise of the veteran animators. The older elephants, caricatured as gossipy women, feature fine animation by Bill Tytla and John Lounsbery. Perhaps the most original sequence in the movie is the one in which Dumbo and his friend Timothy Mouse get drunk and see pink elephants. This leads directly to the scenes in which Dumbo learns that he can fly, a discovery which is prompted by the raucous encouragement of Ward Kimball's quartet of hipster crows.

Disney had begun preparatory work on *Bambi* as early as 1937, before the release of *Snow White,* but for various reasons it did not reach movie theaters until 1942. The prevailing mood of this film (until the climax, at least) is one of lyricism. Humor is blended with

Preparatory work for *Bambi* included elaborate studies of animals in action

Dumbo

Dumbo follows the career of a young elephant from the night he is delivered by stork at the winter quarters of the circus to the day he learns he can fly and to his "arrival" as a national celebrity

the lyricism, but it is humor of a very gentle variety and does not interrupt the mood. The forest becomes a character in the movie, every bit as important as any of the animals. Its response to weather (as in the raindrop sequence with its effective use of multiplane shots) and to season (as in the autumn montage) is as much a part of the story as any of the things that happen to Bambi and his friends. Much of the credit for this should go to Tyrus Wong, who keyed the background styling.

Great emphasis was placed on naturalism in the making of *Bambi*. Special art classes—an extension of the existing training program—were instituted so that Rico LeBrun could instruct the animators in the finer points of drawing animals. Real deer were kept on the lot as models for the artists. Books of photographic studies and innumerable model sheets were compiled, along with analyses of animal action and thousands of feet of live-action material to be used for reference.

Technically, *Bambi* has a great deal to commend it. Much patient work went into it and we might single out the contributions of the art direction team, headed by Tom Codrick, and the animation of Frank Thomas, Milt Kahl, Ollie Johnston, Eric Larson, and Retta Scott. But, for all the effort and skill, *Bambi* is ultimately unsatisfying—especially by the standards Disney had set for himself in his earlier features. The artists cannot be faulted. The problem lies with the interpretation, perhaps with the script itself. In earlier Disney films—both shorts and features—the fact that animals take on human characteristics and have human voices is not disturbing, since they exist in a world of their own which is governed by its own rules. We are not surprised, for instance, when Pinocchio is seduced from the straight and narrow by a fox and a cat, for they are clearly caricatures of human types and the story

Bambi

In *Bambi*, Disney artists aimed for a
degree of naturalism quite unprecedented
in the history of the animated film

unfolds in a fantastic dimension which we recognize as a metaphor
for reality rather than as a naturalistic portrayal. Even the animals
and birds in *Snow White* do not disturb us by their intelligent
behavior. Within the framework of the fairy tale it seems quite
acceptable, and only relatively small demands are made on
them—they are not even asked to speak. Prior to *Bambi*, Disney's
use of humanized animals had always been within the limits of
established idioms.

Bambi, however, is something quite different. This film aims
for a kind of naturalism which falls outside the borders of fantasy
and fairy tale—it presents an owl on friendly terms with baby
rabbits who, in the real forest, would be his victims, and we are
asked to believe in deer that speak the language and share the
emotions of the humans who are supposed to be their enemies. It is
very difficult to reconcile these contradictions.

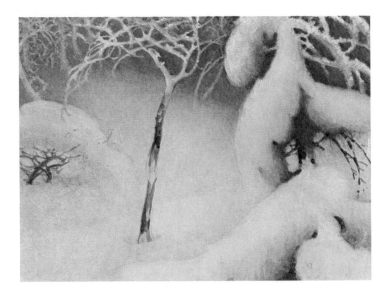

Background treatments for *Bambi* were
conceived to sustain a lyrical mood

The most sympathetic characters are those, like Thumper the
rabbit and Flower the skunk, who are used mostly for humorous
relief. They seem to belong to the Disney mainstream and work
well in those terms.

Yet despite its shortcomings, *Bambi* is an important movie.
Along with the four preceding feature films and the short cartoons
of the thirties, it gave the Studio a tremendous reservoir of idioms
and techniques. The Disney artists could now handle everything,
from the broad stylization of Mickey or Goofy to the naturalism of
Bambi's mother. They had learned how to create any atmosphere
they might need, and the multiplane camera allowed them to use
space in new and complicated ways. The Disney paint laboratory
had developed hundreds of new colors to extend the possibilities of
animation in still another way.

9 Interruptions and Innovations

Victory Through Air Power, 1943, argued the virtues of strategic bombing. *Der Fuehrer's Face*, released that same year, took the form of a nightmare in which Donald Duck found himself working in a Nazi munitions factory

America's entry into the war had an almost immediate effect on Disney Productions. In December, 1941, part of the Studio was commandeered by the military authorities as quarters for seven hundred members of an antiaircraft unit. They took over the sound stage for use as a repair shop and stayed for several months.

Before very long, someone in the Navy realized that animation could be of great value in the presentation of training material. The Studio soon received a series of contracts from military and government agencies and commenced production of short instructional films. The variety of material treated can be suggested by listing some of these wartime titles. The 1942 subjects included *Aircraft Carrier Landing Signals, Aircraft Production Processes, Battle of Britain, Food Will Win the War*, and a number of aircraft-identification films. Among later efforts were *The Battle of China, British Torpedo Plane Tactics, Air Masses and Fronts, Defense Against Invasion, Rules of the Nautical Road, Automotive Electricity for Military Vehicles, Basic Map Reading, Tuning Transmitters, Fundamentals of Artillery Weapons*, and *The Winged Scourge* (which concerned itself not with the Luftwaffe but with malaria-bearing mosquitoes). Since economy was at a premium in these productions, extensive and clever use was made of limited animation (limited in that camera movements and other basic devices were substituted for full animation wherever possible). A more ambitious project was *Victory Through Air Power*, a feature-length film presenting the strategic bombing theories of Major Alexander de Seversky.

The two most important commercial releases of this period—*Saludos Amigos* and *The Three Caballeros*—were themselves indirect products of the war. Europe had been in turmoil since September, 1939, which meant that Hollywood's chief overseas market was wiped out, except for Great Britain and some small neutral countries. Everybody, from the State Department down, was anxious that other markets be expanded, and the most obvious target for this expansion was Latin America (it was no accident that stars like Carmen Miranda rose to prominence at this time). In 1941, Nelson Rockefeller, then Coordinator for Latin American Affairs at the State Department, invited Disney to make a good-will trip to Argentina, Peru, Chile, and Brazil. Disney was not interested

Saludos Amigos

The 1943 package film *Saludos Amigos* included the story of Pedro the mail plane and introduced Donald's friend José Carioca

in a simple hand-shaking tour but suggested instead that it be combined with a film project. The State Department agreed to underwrite four short films to the extent of $50,000 each.

Disney and his wife, along with a group of Studio artists, made the trip and came back with a mass of material which was grafted onto other ideas that had been developed at the Studio. Four separate shorts were produced, but it was decided that it would be advantageous to release them as a single package. They were dovetailed into some documentary footage that had been shot on the tour and released under the title *Saludos Amigos*.

The first of the four animated segments is "Lake Titicaca," which illustrates the adventures of Donald Duck in the High Andes. It has some good moments but is no better than any of half-a-dozen Duck cartoons from this period. The second segment, "Pedro," is more interesting, telling the story of a little mail plane which must carry its cargo across the mountains despite foul weather. A remarkable sense of space and depth was achieved for the flying sequences, and both backgrounds and animation are excellent. The third segment, "Aquarela do Brasil," is the most memorable, featuring José Carioca, an energetic parrot who introduces Donald Duck to Rio's Copacabana Beach and to the samba. The action is lively and is helped along by some imaginative effects animation, but what makes "Aquarela" so distinctive is the fact that it has a real Latin flavor and heralds a mood that was new to Disney movies. The final animated segment is "El Gaucho Goofy," starring the Goof as a displaced cowboy. It is amusing but by no means innovative.

Saludos Amigos was released in February, 1943. Two years later, *The Three Caballeros* appeared. In many respects a sequel, it also was aimed at the Latin American market and, like its predecessor, featured a combination of live action and animation. Taken as a whole, it is a disappointing movie—patchy and with no highlights to compare with the best things in *Saludos Amigos*. Donald and Carioca have some lively moments and are joined by a Mexican rooster called Panchito, who sports a large sombrero and an itchy trigger finger. Their energy is not enough to offset the lackluster character of segments such as "The Cold-blooded Penguin" and "The Flying Gauchito."

The package film was not an ideal format for Disney artists to work with, but it did have an economic advantage which remained a major factor as the war came to an end. Reorganization was necessary, and it was important that the Studio have feature-length productions in the theaters to bring in revenues for future programs. A true animated feature would have taken too long to make and would have eaten up too much of the reserves at this point, so other solutions had to be found. *Saludos Amigos* and *The Three Caballeros* had shown Disney that the package movie was one

The animated portions of *Song of the South*, 1946, brought the animals of the Uncle Remus stories to life

Make Mine Music: "After You've Gone" is one of the segments from this 1946 package film

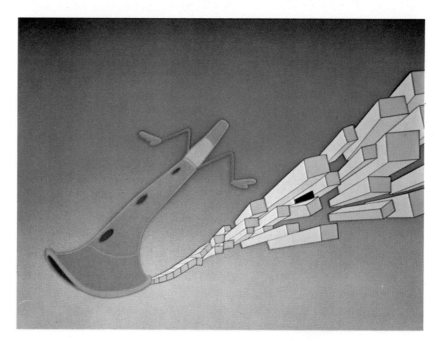

Released in 1949, *The Adventures of Ichabod and Mr. Toad* combined screen adaptations of two famous stories

solution, and three more were produced—*Make Mine Music* (1946), *Fun and Fancy Free* (1947), and *Melody Time* (1948).

In 1946 Disney released *The Adventures of Ichabod and Mr. Toad*. This picture falls somewhere between being a package film and a true feature, consisting of two distinct and separate stories which are linked only by the fact that the hero of each segment is prone to disaster. The "Toad" episode is based on Kenneth Grahame's *The Wind in the Willows* and is enlivened by good character animation and some lively art direction. Unfortunately, the story is too compressed for any of the personalities to be fully explored. All the action is there, but not the leisurely pace of the original (it seems that Disney had intended the story to furnish a feature-length film but was forced to settle for this compromise version).

The tale of Ichabod, based on Washington Irving's *The Legend of Sleepy Hollow*, is narrated by Bing Crosby. *The Adventures of Ichabod and Mr. Toad* is not a great movie, but it was a definite step toward regaining past glories.

The Studio was still producing short cartoons on a regular basis. (It continued to do so until 1956.) Donald and Goofy were now the biggest stars. Formulas had been devised for them which made them easy to write for (Donald's bad temper and the Goof's ineptness provided endless gag possibilities). Mickey still made occasional appearances, but he was now used almost exclusively as a straight man. Important newcomers were Chip and Dale, a pair of highly competitive and occasionally pugnacious chipmunks who were often pitted against Donald, driving him to distraction (he had several other antagonists, including a musical bee and an athletic beetle).

On occasion, short subjects were accorded rather special

116

TOP: the 1950 short *Motor Mania* is one of several that take an ironic look at the habits of the American driver.
CENTER: *Two Chips and a Miss*, 1952, a typical outing for Chip and Dale.
BOTTOM: *Toot, Whistle, Plunk, and Boom*, 1953, is an experimental short made in Cinemascope

treatment, as was the case with *Toot, Whistle, Plunk, and Boom* (1953), the first Cinemascope cartoon. Devised by Ward Kimball, it is a highly stylized history of music which makes use of a novel sound track—very simplified and lacking the lush orchestration that had become standard. Its use of limited animation, along with the widened format, gave it a very distinctive character. A similar subject from the same year, *Adventures in Music: Melody,* was used as an experiment in 3D animation.

Meanwhile, in 1950, Disney released his first true animated feature since 1942. This was *Cinderella,* and it was a success both at the box office and as a piece of film-making.

In spirit it harks back to *Snow White,* though with added surface glamour and with a greater reliance on gag routines. An interesting variety of treatments is brought to the human characters. Cinderella, her stepmother, and the Prince are treated more or less naturalistically, while the ugly stepsisters, the Fairy Godmother, the King, and the Duke are essentially caricatures. Surprisingly, they work very well together. The animal characters are excellent. Lucifer the cat is a splendid villain and the mice (who, thanks to the vocal talents of Jim MacDonald, speak a kind of pidgin Latin) are consistently entertaining. The backgrounds for *Cinderella* are less distinctive than those which added so much to *Snow White* and *Pinocchio* (Albert Hurter had died some years earlier and his influence was greatly missed), but they are more than adequate, establishing a kind of French Provincial look in the early scenes.

Cinderella succeeds because it remains faithful to the spirit of the original while embroidering it with the kind of business that Disney understood better than anyone else. The next feature, *Alice in Wonderland,* failed because it did not capture the sophisticated atmosphere of Lewis Carroll's book and also lacks, except in a few isolated scenes, the authority of the Disney touch. Disney had first talked of animating *Alice* while *Snow White* was still in production (his interest in the subject goes back even further, of course, to Kansas City and *Alice's Wonderland*). He worked at the idea on and off for years before it finally reached the screen in 1951, but for some reason he never came completely to grips with it. Translating Carroll's highly intellectual verbal humor into visual terms was no easy thing, and *Alice* is perhaps the weakest of Disney's animated features. Occasionally there is a sharp piece of Surrealistic visual invention, and there is one excellent sequence—the Mad Hatter's tea party, which is greatly enlivened by the voice talents of Ed Wynn and Jerry Colonna.

Disney blamed the failure of the film on the fact that Alice lacked "heart." Whatever the reasons for its failure, about 1971, much to the amazement of the Disney front office, requests for

Cinderella

Cinderella was Disney's first true animated feature since *Bambi*. Released in 1950, it recaptured much of the spirit of the early features, modified by a new lightness of touch and an emphasis on surface glamour

Alice in Wonderland

Released in 1951, *Alice in Wonderland* had
some brilliant visual touches but failed to
capture the flavor of Lewis Carroll's story

Peter Pan

Disney's version of *Peter Pan*, 1953, is a
generally entertaining interpretation of Sir
James Barrie's stage classic

Lady and the Tramp

Released in 1955, *Lady and the Tramp* was the first animated feature made in Cinemascope. More significantly, it broke new ground in terms of subject matter, setting a more informal tone for future Disney movies

rentals of the 16mm print of *Alice* began to pour in from all over the country. The demand was chiefly from college film societies, but private individuals accounted for a respectable proportion of the rentals. At the Lincoln Center Disney Film Retrospective held in New York during the summer of 1973, the two scheduled showings of *Alice* were the first performances to sell out, and three additional ones were immediately added. This indisputable evidence of the film's new appeal provided the needed impetus, and *Alice* was rereleased in theaters throughout the country in the spring of 1974.

Peter Pan, released in 1953, is an altogether more satisfactory picture. With the exception of Nana, the St. Bernard, and the crocodile, all the main characters are human or have human characteristics (as is the case with Tinker Bell and the Mermaids). We have discussed the special problems involved in animating the human form, but this movie shows just how expert Disney's artists had become at handling them. As in *Cinderella,* they mixed naturalism and caricature without allowing them to clash.

The year 1955 saw the release of *Lady and the Tramp,* Disney's first animated feature to make use of the Cinemascope format. It is innovative in another way too. Set in the recent past, *Lady and the Tramp* deals with a kind of subject matter that had not been encountered at the Studio before, taking us for the first time into a world which is not far removed from our own. *Dumbo,* it is true, is set in the present, but its circus milieu makes it a special case, the atmosphere of the Big Top setting it apart from the everyday world. *Lady and the Tramp* is set largely in the suburbs of a medium-size American city in the early years of the century, an environment compounded from a vernacular that is still familiar today.

Considering the problems of layout, space, and depth inherent in the wide-screen medium, *Lady and the Tramp* turned out remarkably well. The animators did a good job of grafting human personalities onto the main characters without losing the nuances of dog behavior that were necessary if the story was to be convincing. Interaction between dogs and humans is neatly handled and there are some well-executed action scenes (Tramp killing the rat is one that springs to mind, and Jock and Trusty intercepting the dogcatcher's wagon at the climax of the movie). The film's humor is low-keyed—outright gag routines would have destroyed the atmosphere—and it features some agreeable songs.

Lady and the Tramp was followed by another wide-screen feature—one that began with high hopes and ended in disaster.

Sleeping Beauty was conceived as the most spectacular of the postwar productions. Eyvind Earle devised background stylings based on Early Renaissance paintings, and the characters were designed to blend with these settings. Much care was lavished on

Six years in the making, *Sleeping Beauty*, 1959, marked a temporary return to the world of the fairy tale

planning scenes to make the best possible use of the Technirama 70mm format, and the multiplane camera was to be used extensively. Because of other projects, however, *Sleeping Beauty* took six years to complete. It finally reached movie theaters in January, 1959, and was greeted with a pervasive lack of enthusiasm.

In all fairness, the film has some excellent moments. The evil fairy, Maleficent, is a well-conceived character and gets sterling support from her army of goons. The Good Fairies are entertaining, and there is some splendid effects animation, especially toward the climax, when the Prince is fighting his way to the castle, facing a fire-breathing dragon and a forest of thorns. Against this must be set the fact that the hero and heroine remain the merest of ciphers throughout the movie—their personalities are wholly compounded from clichés. Also, the backgrounds—though interesting in themselves—are so busy that they distract from the characters.

We must consider the possibility that the time for fairy tales was past. *Lady and the Tramp* had pointed to another direction that Disney animation could take. The artists had proved that they were not limited to the more traditional forms of fantasy, and the animated features of the sixties would make this still more evident.

10 Later Animation

As far as animation was concerned, new formats like Cinemascope and Technirama 70 proved to be more trouble than they were worth. The next feature, *One Hundred and One Dalmatians,* made use of a technical innovation which was to make a more lasting impact. During the fifties Ub Iwerks, now in charge of special processes at the Studio, had been experimenting with Xerox photography as an aid to animation. By 1959 he had modified a Xerox camera to transfer animators' drawings directly to cels, thus eliminating the inking process and preserving much of the spontaneity of the drawings. As a time (and money) saver, this was of enormous importance to the Studio, and it had a major effect on the way future Disney animation would look, since the distinctive character of the Xerox cels would influence the art direction. The Xerox line would now be employed for most backgrounds, too, so that there would be no stylistic clash between character and setting. This has meant that recent Disney films have had a more linear and graphic look—quite different from the tonal renderings that were so typical of the earlier features.

One Hundred and One Dalmatians represents more than technical innovation. It is a very good movie. The new process made the artists' task easier and left them free to concentrate on the real substance of the film—character development and story. Set in the present, the plot unfolds in London and the surrounding English countryside. The opening sequences, in which true love finds a way, are a little weak, but the moment Cruella de Vil—the villainess of the piece—enters the picture, the pace picks up and never flags again. The treatment is loose and witty, with plenty of action and laughs, and the viewer is given no chance to lose sympathy for the heroes as the story builds steadily to a fitting climax.

The dogs and other animals are, as in *Lady and the Tramp,* human surrogates and work very well as such. Perhaps the most interesting animation in the film, however, is reserved for the humans. They are drawn with a looseness which was new to Disney features, no attempt being made to imitate photographic reality. Elbows and knees are not always where they should be according to anatomy books, but everything works. Roger and Anita, the owners of the Dalmatians, are believable if not memorable, while Horace

One Hundred and One Dalmatians

This film provides fast-moving entertainment and many good touches, including "quotations" from old Disney cartoons (seen on television), and Cruella de Vil, who is perhaps the best villainess in Disney's postwar movies

The Sword in the Stone

Released in 1963, *The Sword in the Stone* brought to the screen Disney's version of the boyhood of King Arthur

and Jasper, the two thugs, are excellent, projecting just the right degree of malicious stupidity. But the real triumph of the film is Cruella. Animated by Marc Davis, she is the most sophisticated of Disney bad guys (the plot revolves around her desire for a coat made from the skins of Dalmatian puppies). Her face is a blend of death mask and fashion plate, perfectly expressing her character, which is at the same time evil and laughable.

Unfortunately, the next animated feature was not one of the Studio's better efforts. Released in December, 1963, *The Sword in the Stone* presents the boyhood of King Arthur, concentrating on his education at the hands of Merlin the Magician. The film totally misses the tone of T. H. White's story and, while there are some amusing set pieces and the animation is as accomplished as ever, character development is weak. Merlin, instead of being awesome, is presented as a bungling nincompoop, thus destroying the essence of the plot.

The Jungle Book was the last animated film that Walt Disney ever produced. In the late fall of 1966, a medical checkup revealed

The Jungle Book

Voice talents—including those of George
Sanders, Phil Harris, Louis Prima, Sterling
Holloway, and Sebastian Cabot—played
an important part in this film

The Aristocats

A moonlit night in Paris, from the finished production, and one of Ken Anderson's sketches for *The Aristocats*

that he was suffering from advanced cancer of the lung. One lung was removed, but six weeks later, on December 15, he died in his room at St. Joseph's Hospital in Burbank, directly across the street from the Studio. He was sixty-five years old. *The Jungle Book* was not quite finished, and the Disney artists were left with the painful task of completing it without him. Happily, *The Jungle Book* is a film that he would have been proud of. It takes great liberties with Kipling's original, but these are justified by the end result.

The Jungle Book was the first feature film of which it can be said that the voice talents were more than just appropriate. Phil Harris, George Sanders, Sterling Holloway, Louis Prima, Verna Felton, Pat O'Malley, and Sebastian Cabot were chosen to speak for the animals of Kipling's jungle—all of them actors whose voices had distinct personalities that would to a large extent dictate the approach the animators would have to take. We have remarked

Winnie the Pooh and the Blustery Day

Featuring Tigger, Eeyore, and, of course, Pooh Bear, *Winnie the Pooh and the Blustery Day*, 1968, is a charming adaptation of an A.A. Milne story

before that animators think of themselves as actors, and now they took on the challenging task of matching their own skills to the performances of the live actors.

Before he died, Walt Disney had—on the strength of a board of drawings by Ken Anderson—given the go-ahead for the next feature project, which appeared in 1970 as *The Aristocats*. This film blends the vernacular style of *One Hundred and One Dalmatians* with *The Jungle Book*'s developments in voice characterization, and the result is a delightful comedy that has enjoyed great popularity.

An aristocratic cat named Duchess (Eva Gabor) and her three kittens become the objects of the evil designs of their mistress's butler. Stranded in the French countryside, they are befriended by an alley cat called O'Malley (Phil Harris again). The film follows their adventures as they make their way back to Paris, only to be confronted once more by the black-hearted butler. This time the villain gets his just deserts and Duchess and O'Malley live happily ever after (the story line is reminiscent of *Lady and the Tramp*).

Winnie the Pooh and the Honey Tree (1966) and *Winnie the Pooh and the Blustery Day* (1968) are a pair of admirable featurettes made during this same period. Apart from Americanizing some of A. A. Milne's characters, the Disney artists dealt very capably with the difficult task of translating the atmosphere of the original to the screen. The second film is especially good, with imaginative animation of the book itself (wind and rain threaten to blow or wash the words from the pages). Most of the characters are well conceived, with Tigger perhaps the outstanding success.

At least five of the postwar features—*Cinderella, Lady and the Tramp, One Hundred and One Dalmatians, The Jungle Book,* and *The Aristocats*—are excellent, each of them moving toward a more informal kind of entertainment. If we put these together with the first five features and the best shorts of the thirties and forties, we have an extraordinary body of work. Walt Disney's achievement can hardly be overstated. He took a marginal branch of the entertainment industry, transformed it into an art form, and then went on to make a major contribution to the history of the cinema.

What makes this all the more remarkable is the fact that it represents only one aspect of his career.

There is a degree of overlap in the production of Disney animated features. Before one is finished, the next is already in a fairly advanced stage of planning. Several possible stories will be investigated and one selected as the most likely candidate. Almost everyone will be involved in this process, with the director, Woolie Reitherman, and his top animators very much to the fore. But the

Robin Hood

Like many other Disney films, *Robin Hood* uses animals to caricature human types

man who has the greatest responsibility at this stage is Ken Anderson, whose wide experience in layout, story, character design, and art direction makes him an excellent choice for the task of developing new projects. While *The Aristocats* was still on the boards, Anderson was exploring possibilities for the next film. Studio executives favored a "classic" subject for the upcoming movie. Ken Anderson suggested a new treatment of the Robin Hood legend, and everyone was enthusiastic.

Once an overall approach and the broad outlines of the story had been decided on, the Studio began to look around for voice talent to fit the characters, and a notable array of acting ability was assembled. Peter Ustinov was signed to play Prince John, a vain and insecure lion who is the pathetic villain of the piece. Terry-Thomas was cast as the snake Sir Hiss, Prince John's constant and obsequious companion. Robin Hood, portrayed as a fox, is played by Brian Bedford, and Phil Harris was featured once again, this time as the voice of Little John. Other talents concerned include those of Andy Devine, Pat Buttram, and country and western singer Roger Miller.

The first animator to work in earnest on *Robin Hood* was Ollie Johnston. While the remainder of the staff was still engaged on another project, Johnston began to develop the character of Prince John, building on Ustinov's voice track and Ken Anderson's character sketches. (Anderson had turned, for inspiration, to the cartoon segments of *Song of the South*—recalling that everyone had enjoyed working on that picture and theorizing that it represented "the kind of thing we do best.") In delineating the personality of the decadent lion, Johnston was very much guided by Ustinov's interpretation of the character—so much so, in fact, that it is impossible to watch Prince John's scenes without seeing a strong hint of the actor's features under the animal's shaggy mane. Johnston added touches of his own, rounding the character out; then the other animators joined him, making their own contributions. No one person is totally responsible for the overall concept of Prince John. His character is blended from the contributions of a dozen different people.

Further projects are already being planned. In one important respect, then, this discussion of Disney animation must remain incomplete, since we are talking about a going concern. Just how much of a future there is for animated features depends on the extent to which younger artists can be attracted to a craft which demands a long and exacting apprenticeship. The present dynasty of animators can carry the weight of production for a time, but there is an urgent need for reinforcements.

For the time being, however, the organization that Walt Disney built continues to occupy its unique position in the motion picture industry.

3. Live-action films...

11 Actors and Animals

Walt Disney's greatest contribution to the motion picture industry was the genius he brought to the art of animation. Since World War II, however, his Studio has become equally well known for its live-action movies and its television shows. Disney had had limited experience in live-action production stretching back to his Kansas City days (the Alice Comedies had involved the filming of a number of juvenile performers), but the release in 1941 of *The Reluctant Dragon* can be seen as a significant departure from the mainstream of the Studio's productions. At one level this film is a documentary about Disney animation, but it becomes more than that as the result of a linking narrative device which has Robert Benchley visiting the Burbank premises with the intention of selling a movie idea (he performs this chore under duress, prompted by his domineering wife). When Benchley arrives at the main gate, he is given a pass and a uniformed escort who is to conduct him into the presence of Mr. Disney. Managing to elude his guide, he finds himself involved in all kinds of Studio activities—story conferences, art classes, recording sessions, and the like. Friendly animators show him the secrets of their craft while a charming young lady introduces him to the magic of the paint laboratory and the multiplane camera, also demonstrating to him how sound effects are produced. Eventually Benchley does reach Disney, only to discover that the idea he is trying to sell has already been made into a movie. These incidents are punctuated by short cartoon inserts, including one called "The Reluctant Dragon," and all kinds of tricks are introduced to help the narrative along (at one point the movie changes from black-and-white to Technicolor). *The Reluctant Dragon* is something of a curiosity. Unpretentious and charming, it gives us an interesting if somewhat fictionalized account of the Disney Studio during its golden age.

Segments of live-action footage began to find their way into package films such as *The Three Caballeros* and *Fun and Fancy Free*, but the real breakthrough came with *Song of the South*, released in 1946, the first Disney film that used a full complement of professional actors to tell an entirely fictional story. It also capitalized on the reputation of Disney animation by including three cartoon episodes, but from the point of view of future developments it was more significant that the live-action sequences

Although it includes segments of animation, *Song of the South*, released in 1946, is primarily a live-action costume drama. Set in the Deep South, the film stars James Baskett as Uncle Remus

were well conceived and executed. *Song of the South* displays the confident professionalism one expects from Hollywood movies of that period.

A little more than two years later, in January, 1949, Disney released *So Dear to My Heart*, which, like *Song of the South*, starred Bobby Driscoll and Luana Patten as children in nineteenth-century rural America. A minimal amount of animation was used in this film; for all practical purposes it is a live-action production telling the story of a boy and his pet sheep. Lacking a central figure as strong as James Baskett's Uncle Remus, the film is less memorable than *Song of the South*, but it is another well-made movie with a good deal to recommend it.

The next phase in the development of Disney live-action production came about largely as the result of a historical accident. Because of postwar monetary restrictions, a sizable amount of Disney capital, the product of accrued royalties, was frozen in the United Kingdom. This meant that funds which were not available to the company in the United States could be used in the British Isles. On the advice of his brother Roy, Walt Disney decided to use these funds to make live-action films in England. The fruits of this venture were four costume dramas—*Treasure Island, The Story of Robin Hood and His Merrie Men, The Sword and the Rose,* and *Rob Roy, the Highland Rogue*—which were released between 1950 and 1954.

All four of these films can be described as unpretentious, well-told, satisfying adventure stories. *Treasure Island*, the first and probably the best of the series, is based on Robert Louis Stevenson's classic novel and is highlighted by Robert Newton's mesmerizing performance as Long John Silver—although even without Newton the movie would have had enough good qualities to ensure its success. The screenplay is simple but effective, Byron Haskin's direction is clean and straightforward, the acting is good throughout, and the action sequences are handled with vigor and style.

The same general virtues are to be found in the other British adventure stories. These films, which featured performers such as Richard Todd, Jack Hawkins, James Robertson Justice, and Glynis Johns, introduced Disney to the reservoir of acting talent that was available in London, one he would draw upon often in future projects.

At some point soon after the war, Disney seems to have conceived the idea of making a film about the pioneer spirit. He realized that the last frontier within the political orbit of the United States was Alaska. The conventional Hollywood approach to a subject such as the last frontier would have involved a couple of major stars, a director with a reputation for handling epic subjects, and a big budget, but Disney was not bound by convention and his approach

Treasure Island

Starring Robert Newton and Bobby Driscoll, *Treasure Island*, 1949, was the first in a series of costume dramas made in the British Isles

Seal Island

Seal Island was the first of Disney's True Life Adventures. It created at one stroke a completely new genre—the general-interest nature film

was quite different. He got in touch with a man by the name of Al Milotte, who owned a camera store in Alaska. Milotte and his wife, Elma, had experience with 16mm filming, and Disney asked them to shoot some footage for him, without being very specific about what it should be.

Al Milotte had for some time wanted to visit the Pribilof Islands—bleak rocks in the Bering Sea—to film the thousands of fur seals that migrate there annually to mate and raise their pups. He asked Disney if this would be of interest. Disney wired him to go ahead, and soon footage of seals began to arrive at the Studio. According to James Algar, who was one of those entrusted with the task of structuring this footage, it was difficult at first to make much sense of the material they were screening, but Disney saw something that held his interest. The seals were acting out a primitive rite that had been repeated for thousands of years. The problem was to present this rite in dramatic terms that would be readily understood by a theater audience. The Disney staff began to research the subject and to put together the story of the seals' life cycle; eventually they developed a clear pattern of events which could provide a usable framework for a movie. The film sent by the Milottes was tailored to this story, and the result was a twenty-seven-minute picture titled *Seal Island,* released in 1949.

Seal Island was not an easy movie to sell. Distributors could not envision what market there would be for it, but eventually a Pasadena theater gave the film a short run. Audience response was good, and *Seal Island* was nominated for an Academy Award as the best short subject of the year. The film won the Oscar and Disney's True Life Adventure Series was successfully launched. In searching

The Living Desert

One of the most successful of the True Life Adventures, *The Living Desert*, 1953, is a feature-length production marked by spectacular nature photography

for the last frontier, Disney had discovered a new frontier—nature.

Between 1950 and 1960, more than a dozen True Life Adventures were produced by the Studio. The two-reel format introduced by *Seal Island* was used for most subjects—titles include *Beaver Valley, Nature's Half Acre, The Olympic Elk, Bear Country, Prowlers of the Everglades*, and *Water Birds*. Six feature-length films were also made—*The Living Desert, The Vanishing Prairie, The African Lion, White Wilderness, Secrets of Life*, and *Jungle Cat.*

The Milottes were involved in several of these productions but many other cameramen also contributed to the True Life Adventures—most of them trained naturalists. The same basic formula was used for all the films. A subject was chosen and crews dispatched to the appropriate locations to gather footage (films such as *Secrets of Life* demanded laboratory filming rather than outdoor work). The raw material was sent back to Hollywood and edited into usable form by a team headed by James Algar, Winston Hibler, and Ben Sharpsteen. The producers relied on the audience's tendency to identify with the animals at an emotional level, so animal behavior was interpreted in human terms. The structure of each movie and the commentary that accompanies it were conceived with this end in mind.

The True Life Adventures have sometimes been criticized for this subjectivity, and to some extent this criticism is justified. Certainly the material is presented in such a way that we are not given much chance to interpret it for ourselves. At the same time, we must take into consideration the fact that these films were not

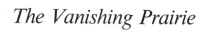

The Vanishing Prairie

The African Lion

A specially constructed camera truck allowed Al and Elma Milotte to shoot extraordinary wildlife footage for *The African Lion*, released in 1955

intended to be scientific documents—they were designed for the enjoyment of a mass audience that was not yet prepared to accept this kind of material without a measure of sweetening.

Spin-offs from the True Life Adventures include the People and Places series and, more significantly, the many later Disney films which blend animal footage with conventional live-action dramas. *Perri*, released in 1957, was the story of a squirrel; its material was similar to that used in the True Life Adventures, but was organized in such a way that it corresponded with the fictional narrative on which the film was based.

12 Davy Crockett, Other Heroes, and Mary Poppins

Starring Fess Parker and Buddy Ebsen, *Davy Crockett* was the great success of Disney's first television season

As early as the 1930s, Walt Disney had been aware of the potential importance of television—perhaps because Mickey Mouse cartoons were used in early tests of transmitting equipment—and he was careful to retain television rights to all his films. By the late 1940s, the other major studios were seriously worried about the impact the new medium was having on theater attendance, and tried to recoup some of their losses by selling the home-screen rights to their backlog of productions. Disney was almost alone in holding out against the short-term advantages of this course of action.

Having retained television rights to all his films, Disney had a great reservoir of past productions to draw on, but a good deal of fresh material was prepared for the initial season in 1954. The programs were presented by the American Broadcasting Company. Disney, although not entirely enthusiastic about television, was anxious to go ahead with the plans for building Disneyland, and in return for the prestige of a Disney series, ABC agreed to make a major investment in the park. The new series was, quite appropriately, titled *Disneyland*. Bill Walsh, series producer, recalls how almost at once they came up with a hit of quite stunning magnitude: "We were planning to do a series on American folk heroes—like Johnny Appleseed, Daniel Boone, and Big Foot Wallace—and the first one we picked out, by dumb luck, was Davy Crockett. At that time he was considered just one more frontiersman. We shot it down in Tennessee and when we got the film back to the Studio, we found we didn't have quite enough footage for three sixty-minute shows. So Walt said, 'Why don't you take some drawings and stick them all together and give an idea of what the show's going to be about.' So we put the drawings together, sketches of Davy's life, and Walt said, 'Well, that looks kind of dull. Maybe we can get a song to go with them.' " The song was, of course, "The Ballad of Davy Crockett," which—like the television episodes themselves—enjoyed enormous success.

The production was shown in three parts: "Davy Crockett, Indian Fighter," "Davy Crockett Goes to Congress," and "Davy Crockett at the Alamo." Although they were transmitted in

Released in 1954, *20,000 Leagues Under the Sea* was the Studio's most lavish live-action film up to that point. It featured elaborate sets, exotic locations, and spectacular scenes shot in a special water tank

black and white, they were filmed in color, which meant that the footage could advantageously be re-edited for theater release. Seeing this slightly shorter version today, one must observe that it stands up remarkably well, having the same kind of basic strengths as Disney's British costume dramas. The story is told with crispness and a minimum of fuss. Acting and action sequences are excellent. The landscape is used to create atmosphere and the result is a well-constructed, fast-moving adventure story. As biography the plot may be a bit oversimplified, but it remains essentially faithful to the spirit of the legend.

The original *Disneyland* series was broadcast on Wednesday nights and continued in that time slot for four years. For the 1958-59 season the name was changed to *Walt Disney Presents* and the program was moved to Friday evenings. During the 1960-61 season *Walt Disney Presents* was shown on Sunday evenings; in the fall of 1961, the program made a major switch, moving to the NBC television network, where it has kept its Sunday evening time slot. After the move to NBC, all Disney television shows were transmitted in color and the name was changed once again—to *Walt Disney's Wonderful World of Color*. The title was later altered to *Wonderful World of Disney*, but these changes are irrelevant to the central point, which is that the sixty-minute weekly format which Disney developed in 1954 has remained immensely popular—adding up to one of television's all-time success stories.

Another hugely popular Disney show was *The Mickey Mouse Club*, which was launched on October 3, 1955, and televised each weekday afternoon until 1959.

The show developed a pleasant, informal format with which children could identify. The talents of the Mouseketeers were combined with old Disney cartoons and many other kinds of material. Dramatic serials, such as "Spin and Marty," became a popular feature of the program.

Other series such as *Zorro* and *The Mouse Factory* enabled the Disney Studio to retain an important share of the television market. Over the years, it has continued to aim its programing at the most stable area of the market—the family audience—allowing for gradual shifts of taste rather than attempting to make radical changes.

In 1954, the year in which the *Disneyland* television series was launched, the Studio released *20,000 Leagues Under the Sea*, easily its most ambitious live-action picture up to that point

Far removed from its modest predecessors, *20,000 Leagues* was planned as a big-budget movie using major Hollywood stars (Kirk Douglas, James Mason, Paul Lukas, and Peter Lorre) and spectacular special effects.

Swiss Family Robinson

Adapted from Johann Wyss's classic
novel, *Swiss Family Robinson*, 1960,
starred John Mills and featured a
spectacular tree house which later formed
the basis for a popular attraction at both
Disneyland and Walt Disney World

The project demanded elaborate sets and a great deal of trick photography. Much of the action was shot in a large water tank on one of the Disney sound stages; other scenes were filmed in an outdoor tank at the Fox lot, and location work was done in Jamaica and off San Diego. One high spot of the action is a violent fight between the crew of the submarine *Nautilus* and a giant squid—a sequence that called for all the ingenuity the Studio could muster.

The Jules Verne original provided a marvelous basis for a film combining fantasy and adventure. Script and direction were excellent and production values outstanding. James Mason was cast as Captain Nemo—half villain, half hero—bringing a sense of icy rage to the sinister commander of the *Nautilus*. Paul Lukas played an eminent scientist who, along with his apprentice, Peter Lorre, is captured by Nemo. All three characters, in the best Jules Verne tradition, are a little out of the ordinary. Their eccentricity is balanced by the down-to-earth figure of the whaler, played by Kirk Douglas. The whaler is of course brave and strong and handy with a harpoon. More important, his viewpoint is uncomplicated by intellectual aspirations, making him the character with whom most of the potential audience would identify. So far as the protagonists are concerned, *20,000 Leagues Under the Sea* deals in terms of simplifications, but it grips our imagination because it is convincing as a battle of ideas and emotions.

Swiss Family Robinson is yet another major production taken from a classic adventure story. Released in 1960, with John Mills in the starring role, this is the story of an emigrant family shipwrecked on a tropical island. We see how they learn to cope with their unfamiliar environment and how they deal with a band of Oriental pirates.

The Shaggy Dog, released in 1959, was the first of the Studio's zany comedies. It starred Fred MacMurray, and it was followed by other similar vehicles for MacMurray's talents, notably *The Absent Minded Professor,* 1961, and *Son of Flubber,* 1963. The British actress Hayley Mills was featured in several Disney films during this period, including costume pieces such as *Pollyanna* and contemporary comedies like *The Parent Trap.*

The Studio was now enjoying success with a wide variety of live-action productions, and animation was also thriving. The outlook for Disney was very bright, a fact made all the more remarkable because at this time other major studios were experiencing a sharp decline in their fortunes.

In 1964 Disney released *Mary Poppins,* a film which became one of the greatest hits in the history of the motion picture industry. Adapted from P. L. Travers's children's stories, the movie provided

Julie Andrews with a spectacular screen debut and smashed box-office records at home and abroad.

Mary Poppins is a unique movie, imaginative and entertaining. Those who expected a direct adaptation of Mrs. Travers's stories may have been a little disappointed, but it could not have been otherwise. Her delicate fantasies work beautifully in words, but literary artifice does not translate into film without undergoing a considerable change. Bill Walsh and Don DaGradi had to provide the movie with a structure, and they could only do this by altering the raw material to some extent.

Julie Andrews is certainly a more glamorous and youthful version of Mary Poppins than the one we meet in Mrs. Travers's stories. She brings to the character a charm and spark of her own. Her singing voice and dancing ability are great assets, but the key to her performance is her ability to seem prim and proper yet perpetually on the verge of some kind of marvelous insanity. Primness is Mary Poppins's solitary link with everyday reality—a fragile self-discipline that manages, just barely, to impose a modicum of form on the tides of fantasy that flow just below the surface.

Edwardian London is reconstructed with a good feeling for atmosphere, clever use being made both of remarkable special effects and of simple sets that would not seem out of place on the stage of a Broadway theater. Throughout the film, the real and the imaginary are combined in inventive and believable ways, notably, of course, in the scenes that combine live action with animation. In the production of *Mary Poppins,* all of the Studio's resources were pooled to produce a motion picture that probably could not have been made anywhere else.

The sound track is dotted with memorable songs, in particular, "Chim Chim Cher-ee," "Jolly Holiday," "The Life I Lead," "A Spoonful of Sugar," and "Supercalifragilisticexpialidocious." There is at least one dance routine in the best tradition of the Hollywood musical. *Mary Poppins* is, in fact, an extravaganza of the sort that had been fairly plentiful in the thirties and forties, but which seemed to be a lost art in the sixties.

Since *Mary Poppins,* Disney has released a number of interesting live-action films, good examples being *The Happiest Millionaire,* 1967, *The Love Bug,* 1969, *Bedknobs and Broomsticks,* 1971, and *The World's Greatest Athlete,* 1973. Released in December 1974 was *The Island at the Top of the World,* a spectacular Jules Verne type of adventure. One cannot pretend that these films, not to mention the lesser productions that have emerged from the Studio, have made a vital contribution to the history of the cinema, but they do deserve to be treated with more respect than is generally accorded them

Mary Poppins, released in 1964, used all the resources of the Disney Studio, combining live action with animation and featuring startling special effects

One of the most spectacular sequences in *Mary Poppins* is the chimney sweeps' dance, set on the rooftops of London

Walt Disney's position in the pantheon of movie greats results almost entirely from the imagination and vitality he brought to the art of animation. But he was also a very practical man who knew that the kind of operation he ran required a sound financial base. Live-action production has been vital to the fiscal health of the organization. Without these films there might have been no later animated features—perhaps no Disneyland and no Walt Disney World.

4. The Magic Kingdoms...

13 Beyond Film: Disneyland and Walt Disney World

Disneyland grew from an idea that had beem maturing in Disney's head for fifteen or twenty years before it became a physical reality. When his daughters were young, he would take them to local amusement parks and playgrounds, and he said later that those often unsatisfying visits triggered the notion that a park could be devised which would be as entertaining for adults as for their children.

Shortly after the war, Disney's doctor suggested that he find some leisure activity that would give him a chance to escape the pressures of running the Studio, if only for an hour or two a day. Disney had always loved railroads, and this interest was now fanned by the discovery that two of his top animators were already serious railway buffs. One of these was Ollie Johnston, who remembers the beginnings of Disney's enthusiasm:

"I told him I was building a steam engine. He said, 'You are? I always wanted a backyard railroad myself.' So he came out to where we were building mine, in Santa Monica. He came out two or three times and he started to get ideas on how he was going to build his. They started building it here in the shop, several months later. He had this keen setup around his yard with about half a mile of track. He had a real nice thing with a tunnel—it went under his wife's flower garden and he made her sign a contract that said he could put the track there. He had all kinds of bridges and things for it too.

"We'd work at it here at the Studio sometimes. I'd be working on one of my cars, out there in the carpenter's shop, and he'd say, 'Hey, I think I found out where they keep the hardwood.' So he'd show me where I could find some nice scraps of lumber. He built a beautiful, old-fashioned headlight for his engine, and he built all the cars—cattle cars and boxcars. Walt was good with his hands. Roger Brodie was head of the shop then and he kind of guided Walt along.

"The next thing you know, Walt was thinking about putting a railroad around here, at the Studio. There was a guy in Los Gatos who had some engines that were used in the 1915 Pan American Fair in San Francisco, and Walt was thinking of buying those. Then he got to thinking there wasn't enough room here and before long there was a Disneyland."

OVERLEAF: at Walt Disney World, in Florida, Cinderella's Castle is the centerpiece of the Magic Kingdom

When Disneyland opened in
1955, it was surrounded
by orange groves

It's a Small World:
one of the most popular
attractions at both Disneyland
and Walt Disney World

In 1952, Disney set up an organization called WED (the
initials of his own name) to begin planning the park in earnest.
WED consisted, at first, of a handful of designers, mostly co-opted
from the Disney animation department. They were men who
understood how Disney worked and they were well equipped to
interpret his ideas. Plans and models were made for an as yet
unchosen site, and part of the impact of Disneyland may well
derive from the fact that it was planned this way—with Walt's
dream interpreted by his own artists and no attention paid to
potential topographical limitations. As the park began to take
shape on paper, the Stanford Research Institute was called in to
find a site within the greater Los Angeles area. They settled on 160
acres of orange groves in Anaheim, to the south of Los Angeles,
which seemed suitable for a number of reasons.

Disney's overall concept for the park has its own kind of logic,
which has proved extremely effective. His plan called for a railroad
defining the perimeter of the park, with its main station situated
right at the entrance. Once past the station, the visitor would have
to pass down Main Street—a reproduction of the heart of a small
Midwestern town such as Disney himself might have known as a
boy. Entered from a small square on which a town hall and a fire
station were situated, Main Street was calculated to correspond

with one of the archetypes of the American imagination. It was to provide an operating base for many of the concessions, but, more than that, it would establish the right ambiance, so that visitors would be put in a receptive state of mind. Its scale would be slightly less than life-size, to enhance the sense of friendliness and intimacy. Transportation would be available—trams and horse-drawn streetcars—but people on foot would be drawn down Main Street by the imposing edifice at its far end—Sleeping Beauty's Castle—the likes of which has seldom been seen in any Midwestern town.

It would be important to keep people moving in the park, and Disney had an expression which voiced his philosophy in this regard: "You've got to have a wienie at the end of every street." Translated into practical terms, this meant that his planners had to provide a sequence of visual magnets that would keep drawing visitors on to the next attraction. Situated at the hub of the park, the castle would be the biggest of these magnets, and all paths would converge on the traffic circle immediately in front of it.

A visitor who followed a clockwise route from this central feature would find himself, first of all, in Adventureland, next in Frontierland, then in Fantasyland, and finally in Tomorrowland (other possibilities, such as Holiday Land and Lilliputian Land, were considered, then abandoned). Each of these areas would have a specific atmosphere appropriate to its name. Disney characters and references to Disney movies would be found throughout the park.

It was a good plan. It had a sense of structure and continuity which was new to this kind of enterprise, and it capitalized fully on the established Disney image. Everything had been thoughtfully considered and imaginatively developed.

Disneyland was opened on July 17, 1955. Television crews were on hand to record the opening ceremonies, and thirty thousand guests thronged Main Street and explored the farthest reaches of the complex. Millions more saw the opening on their home screens. No entertainment facility had ever enjoyed this kind of publicity, and Disneyland became a national phenomenon overnight. Crowds came flocking through the gate—more than a million between July 18 and September 30, and almost four million during the first complete fiscal year.

Disneyland soon became a regular stopping-off place for all kinds of foreign dignitaries. Walt Disney had built the Versailles of the twentieth century—but it was a Versailles designed for the pleasure of the people. At the time of its inauguration it was not, of course, quite the dense complex that we find today. As yet, no Monorail had been installed, no New Orleans Square divided Adventureland from Frontierland, and many of the most popular

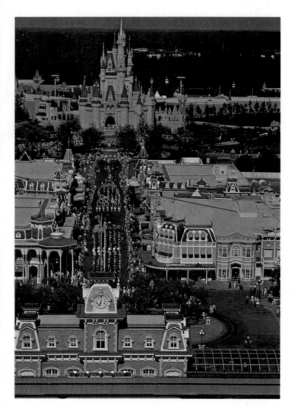

An aerial view of Walt Disney World's Main Street

rides were not even in the planning stage. What existed was an unusual and agreeable environment suitable for further expansion but already providing novel entertainments for both children and adults.

Apart from the originality of its plan, what makes Disneyland radically different from other amusement parks is the fact that it is designed like a movie lot. The skills that go into building film sets are the same skills that went into Main Street and Frontierland. The difference is that a set may consist of facades that open onto nothing, whereas Disneyland's streets are punctuated by doors that give access to rides, entertainments, stores, and restaurants.

The success of Disneyland had persuaded Disney that a second park was desirable. He wanted his new park to serve the Eastern states, and Florida offered the best environment. Its climate—like that of southern California—would permit year-round operation, and the state attracts over twenty million tourists annually. More than three-quarters of these visitors travel by automobile, and as many pass through central Florida. And, because the vast majority of Florida vacationers are from east of the Rockies, the two parks would not be in direct competition.

Disney was not the kind of man who could be satisfied with merely repeating himself, and he conceived his new project as far more than just another Disneyland. It would be a complete vacationland, cushioned from the outside world, providing hotel accommodations and camp sites as well as all kinds of recreational activities, from boating to birdwatching to golf. The project would also include an industrial park designed to showcase American business, and a small community—Lake Buena Vista—which would include both vacation homes and permanent residences. More ambitiously, EPCOT—an experimental prototype community of tomorrow—became part of the plan. Speaking of EPCOT Disney said, "It will take its cue from the new ideas of new technologies emerging from the creative centers of American industry. It will always be introducing and testing and demonstrating new materials and systems." It would be, he said, a place where "people actually live a life they can't find anywhere else in the world today."

In 1964, Disney representatives obtained control of a large area straddling the line separating Orange and Osceola counties in central Florida. Surveying his property from the air, Disney decided that the shores of Bay Lake—its largest natural body of water—was the spot to begin Phase One of the development, and the practicality of this choice was borne out by detailed studies. He died six months before the earth-moving equipment arrived at the site, but he had already supervised the planning of Phase One down to the last detail and laid down general principles for the development of the whole property.

Walt Disney World's Crystal Palace is a spectacular glass-and-steel structure

From a technological point of view, the Hall of Presidents, in Walt Disney World, is probably the most sophisticated attraction Disney engineers have yet built. Featuring lifelike full-scale figures of every American president, its highlight is a speech given by Abraham Lincoln

As scheduled, Walt Disney World was opened by Roy Disney in October, 1971.

Long before he began to build Disneyland, Walt Disney had been a collector of mechanical toys, and these suggested to him the possibility of finding a three-dimensional equivalent for the art of screen animation. In the mid-forties he began to experiment with mechanical puppets, and Ken Anderson worked secretly with him to devise some theatrical settings. Then films were made of Buddy Ebsen dance routines, and Disney engineers (whom he later rebaptized "Imagineers") made a small model of Ebsen which reproduced his movements with reasonable faithfulness. The figure was mounted beneath a proscenium arch above a large console, giving the whole the appearance of a sinister Punch and Judy show, the kind of thing Boris Karloff might have toyed with in some epic of the macabre. At this time, the electronics industry was still in its infancy, and the console had to house cumbersome vacuum tubes as well as many purely mechanical elements—fly wheels and escape mechanisms—with which a clockmaker would be quite familiar. The console was programed by something closely resembling a piano roll—a long strip of paper, punched with patterns of holes, which looped through it and triggered the required responses. The Ebsen puppet worked, but the machinery was too clumsy to suggest any immediate application; for many years it lay neglected, but it has now been restored for an exhibit at Walt Disney World. Later, solid-state technology made animation in the round practical, and Disney engineers developed puppets controlled by what they called "audio-animatronics."

The first audio-animatronic models made were some exotic birds which eventually formed the basis of Disneyland's Tiki Room. The birds, perched among tropical vegetation, put on a little show for visitors, singing and cracking jokes. It was not until 1964, at the New York World's Fair, that the full potential of audio-animatronics was revealed to the public. Disney contributed a number of attractions, including the Ford Motor Company's "Magic Skyway," General Electric's "Progressland," and Pepsi-Cola's "It's a Small World" (the last adapted for both Anaheim and Orlando). The most impressive exhibit, however, was "Great Moments with Mr. Lincoln," which Disney prepared for the Illinois pavilion.

Visitors were confronted with a startlingly lifelike facsimile of the nation's sixteenth president, who rose from his chair and addressed his latter-day countrymen. Lincoln not only talked, he emphasized his thoughts with naturalistic gestures and his eyes raked the audience as though challenging opponents to debate. He shifted his weight from one foot to the other and his expression changed with the sense of his words. He almost seemed to breathe. The impact was extraordinary.

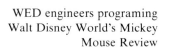

WED engineers programing
Walt Disney World's Mickey
Mouse Review

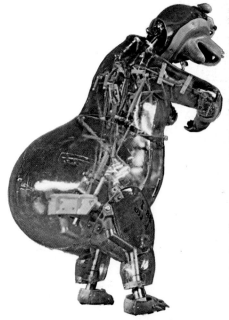

The complexity of the
audio-animatronic figures can
be judged from these
photographs taken at WED
during the preparation of
characters for the Country
Bear Jamboree

This success was not easily won. Indeed, only a few months before the opening of the pavilion it had seemed that Lincoln would never be ready in time. The Lincoln figure was very complex and posed serious control problems. The President smashed his chair and threw mechanical fits that threatened the safety of the men working on him. But Disney was determined that the figure be ready in time, and eventually the power was harnessed.

Equally sophisticated audio-animatronic figures are now featured in many attractions at both Disneyland and Walt Disney World. Pirates of the Caribbean, the Mickey Mouse Review, and both Haunted Mansions offer good examples, but perhaps the most successful ones are to be found in Walt Disney World's Hall of Presidents and at the Country Bear Jamboree, versions of which have been installed in both parks.

Years of experience in the field of screen animation have taught the Disney artists how to use movement with economy. A sense of reality is often best transmitted by suppressing movement—for example, a character may express surprise more effectively by raising an eyebrow than by throwing up his hands. It is such knowledge that has made audio-animatronics so valuable an asset to the parks, for without it, all the engineering skill that goes into these figures would be wasted.

Animation is the most completely controlled form of film-making imaginable. As we have seen in earlier chapters, everything is preplanned. Nothing is left to the temperament of stars, to the day-to-day inspirations of director and cameraman, or to the vagaries of light and weather. Disneyland and Walt Disney World are controlled environments engineered to conform to the principles Disney had developed in making his animated films. All the elements of a movie must be made to complement each other—and this criterion was adapted in designing the parks.

The movie influence is most obvious within the context of individual attractions. The Haunted Mansion, for example, presents us with an example of a ride that unfolds in time in exactly the same way a motion picture does. A movie transports an audience from point A to point Z by means of a carefully structured sequence of visual devices—the camera following the action and the audience traveling with the camera. The camera is, in other words, a moving vehicle which carries the viewer through the plot. In the Haunted Mansion, as in many other attractions at the parks, another kind of vehicle—a car that runs on rails—is substituted for the camera. The visitor is first ushered into a gothic lobby where he finds himself, along with a hundred other people, surrounded by sinister portraits. A disembodied voice issues a few words of warning, then the lights are extinguished and the show begins with a teaser—a device planned to set the atmosphere and to draw the viewer into the unfolding situation. The floor begins to drop and a body suddenly appears, hanging from the ceiling high above. The sinking floor immediately establishes a sense of insecurity, but it has the added practical purpose of bringing visitors down to a basement level where they board the cars that take them through the rest of the show. These cars carry the guests through a sequence of spooky environments, each of which exposes them to a new kind of "supernatural" phenomenon (to describe these would be unfair to future riders). The cars, each wired for stereo sound, are built in such a way that the rider can see only what is directly in front of him. Each car is on a swivel so that it can be turned, by electronic signals, to face just what the designer wants it to face at any particular moment. In this sense, then, it is used exactly like a movie camera. The rider is traveling through a programed show which unfolds in time. The choice of where to look is not his to make—it has already been made by the designer, who determines what will be seen, just as a director determines what the movie patron will see. This degree of control is, of course, limited to certain rides, but everything in the parks is touched by the motion-picture expertise of the Disney organization.

Just as the "theme" parks deal in everything from nostalgia to space technology, so their transportation systems represent a wide variety of types and eras. Main Street is served by tram cars and horse-drawn vehicles, yet a short walk will take you to a stream-lined Monorail. The engines and rolling stock of the railroad circling the park conjure up the golden age of steam, but the People Mover that runs through Tomorrowland is a silent, electrically powered product that belongs entirely to the second half of the twentieth century. Other kinds of transport—from cable cars to river boats—abound, meshed into a complex network made all the more satisfying by the fact that it is so far removed from the mass-transit systems we are accustomed to in the "real" world.

The investment made in each of the major attractions at the parks exceeds the budget of any Broadway show. This is made possible by the fact that one ride alone may be enjoyed by as many as forty thousand people in a single day. The necessity of appealing to so many people—of all ages and from every imaginable background—clearly determines the character of the attractions. Most films or stage performances are aimed at a specific segment of the population which has its own well-defined needs and interests. Disney designers do not have the luxury of trying to satisfy the tastes of only one group—their entertainments must appeal to everyone, and this means that they must work with universal concepts.

Several attractions—Main Street, Frontierland, New Orleans Square, and Liberty Square—capitalize on nostalgia, a sentiment to which everyone responds to some degree. Its opposite, the concept

Disneyland's Haunted Mansion, with its delicate wrought-ironwork, is designed to blend with the architecture of adjacent New Orleans Square

Liberty Square, in Walt Disney World, reproduces the quiet elegance of an American colonial town

The wrought iron and engraved glass of Disneyland's New Orleans Square illustrates the great care taken in reproducing architectural styles for the parks

of progress, is embodied in Tomorrowland. The Jungle Ride, the Swiss Family Robinson's Tree House, and Pirates of the Caribbean all exploit a yearning for the exotic, while the Haunted Mansion and 20,000 Leagues Under the Sea attempt to satisfy our urge to confront the unknown. One could take every feature of the parks and explain its appeal in terms of some instinctive or emotional response common to almost all of us.

This emphasis on the "common factor" does not encourage the designers to indulge in intellectual subtleties, but it does make for a fascinating series of archetypal experiences. A great film or play may broaden the horizons of thousands of people, introducing them to fresh ideas or deepening their understanding of the human condition. The Disney parks have a very different goal. They are designed to satisfy the *existing* imaginative appetites of tens of millions of men, women, and children.

For years, Disneyland was an object of scorn in architectural circles. Many people who had never visited the park deplored its vulgarity and its disregard of textbook precepts. Those who did take the trouble to experience it at first hand were often surprised to discover that Disneyland worked—worked at the very basic level of being a compact architectural complex which could efficiently handle up to fifty thousand people a day. While they paid grudging tribute to Disney's multilayer transportation system, and admitted that the park was rather innovative, the most that the majority of city planners and architects were prepared to say was that Disneyland was a happy accident.

Walt Disney World proved less easy to dismiss, and in fact rapidly attracted a good deal of favorable interest. Taking advantage of the experience gained in developing the first park, and able to plan the entire complex from start to finish, the Disney organization came up with solutions to urban-planning problems that were remarkably similar to those that had been proposed in architectural schools and publications around the world, but had never been put into practice. Disney and his assistants were in a position to implement them. Other planners, hobbled by more conservative clients, watched with considerable envy.

The first difficulty the Disney team had to face was that of turning swamps into building sites without falling back on the expedient of draining the entire area—an unfortunate practice, commonplace in Florida for fifty years or more, that had disastrous effects on the equilibrium of nature. Disney insisted that his planners find a way of creating adequate sites without upsetting the ecological balance.

From the outset one large area—7,500 acres—was set aside as a nature preserve. This tract of swamp and hardwood forest has been kept in its virgin state (only a few poachers have ever ventured into it, hunting for alligators, which are plentiful enough), and it is the

At Walt Disney World, the streamlined Monorail glides past Cinderella's Castle

The Monorail emerges from the vast lobby of
Walt Disney World's A-frame Contemporary Hotel

home of a variety of rare native wildlife, including what are believed to be the last surviving Florida black bears. It is closed to the public, and its untouched character is carefully protected by a team of resident scientists, aided by such organizations as the Audubon Society.

Had Disney decided to follow common practice and drain his entire property, such a preserve would have been impossible, because the change in water level would have altered the terrain irrevocably. Instead, he listened to the best advice and made use of existing high ground wherever possible. A certain amount of drainage was still necessary, but it was kept to a minimum and the water table of the remainder of the forty-three square miles was protected by an elaborate system of levees and sluice gates.

Within this overall framework, extraordinary individual feats of engineering were undertaken. Without disturbing the surrounding landscape, a 200-acre lake was pumped dry, enough white sand from its bed was moved up to the shoreline to provide beautiful beaches, and islands were constructed and planted with palm trees. Then the lake was refilled with clear water free of the dense concentration of tannic acid that had discolored the original water. Thus, a murky Central Florida lake was transformed into something that looked more like a Micronesian lagoon.

Another lake, almost as large, was entirely manmade; in the vicinity of these bodies of water the major architectural developments have been placed.

Visitors to the Magic Kingdom—the chief entertainment area of Walt Disney World—may imagine they are walking on solid ground, but they are in fact promenading on a gigantic deck—rather like the flight deck of an aircraft carrier. Main Street, Cinderella's Castle, and most of the major attractions are built on this deck. Thirty feet below is a kind of gigantic basement—actually the true ground level—which consists of a vast network of corridors wide enough to drive trucks through, offices, repair shops, kitchens, restaurants for employees, the world's largest wardrobe department, and a hundred other things. In a more conventional development, space for all these would have to be provided at surface level. At Walt Disney World, supplies can be moved from one spot to another without visitors to the park seeing a single delivery vehicle. All along the corridors, at ceiling height, are tubes which are part of a sophisticated garbage disposal system. Waste material, deposited at various terminals throughout the park, is sucked through these pipes and disposed of by a nonpolluting incinerator. Walt Disney World also has a very advanced sewage treatment plant; it makes use of living trees and other plants to further purify waste water once it has been treated mechanically and chemically.

Also in the service basement is a computer center that controls almost all the mechanical components of the Magic Kingdom, from the most elaborate of the audio-animatronic exhibits to the tape recorders that provide music for the lobbies of the nearby hotels.

These hotels, the dramatic A-frame "Contemporary," the flashier "Polynesian," and a smaller hotel built alongside one of the golf courses, are assembled entirely from prefabricated steel-frame units manufactured near the site in a plant set up by the United States Steel Corporation. Each unit is slotted into place, fully wired for electricity and with all its plumbing and other services already installed.

The hotels are linked to the Magic Kingdom by the Alweg Monorail, which skirts the lakes, providing spectacular views on all sides. The scale of Walt Disney World allowed Disney to indulge his interest in transportation systems more freely than was possible in Disneyland, and their efficiency is startling—whether one rides the Monorail, the futuristic-looking friction-drive People Mover, or a paddle steamer out of the world of Mark Twain.

Each of the individual innovations at Walt Disney World would, if transplanted to a new housing development or shopping center, provoke considerable interest and comment. More remarkable than any one thing, however—more remarkable than the whole catalogue of experiments—is the overall concept, the Disney master plan.

Toward the end of his life, Walt Disney—the man who started out by trying to tell funny stories with animated rabbits and mice—began to think seriously about our environment and wondering what he could do to improve it. This seems to have been the real motivation behind Walt Disney World. Disney did not have an overwhelming desire to repeat himself by building another entertainment complex. The Magic Kingdom was an old means to a new end, devised to give Disney a chance to try out some ideas that had been crowding their way into his mind. What he looked forward to more than anything else was the planning of EPCOT (Experimental Prototype Community of Tomorrow)—a city that would always be twenty-five years ahead of its time.

It would be naive to suppose that Walt Disney World provides an answer to our problems. It is not a real city—in the sense of Chicago or even Orlando—but it is a valuable testing ground and many of the systems that have already been proven there could be used to improve the quality of our everyday life. Even if EPCOT is never built, Walt Disney World will have given urban planners many valuable pointers.

It is too soon to pass any final historical judgment on Walt Disney World, but we can say that it was the last and most audacious flowering of an extraordinary imagination.